Forgotten Books

The Life of Sir Thomas More

By

William Roper

Published by Forgotten Books 2012

Originally Published 1905

PIBN 1000593565

LIFE OF SIR THOMAS MORE, KNT.

BY HIS SON-IN-LAW

WILLIAM ROPER

WITH A FOREWORD BY

SIR JOSEPH WALTON, KNT.

JUDGE OF THE KING'S BENCH DIVISION

LONDON:
BURNS & OATES,
28 ORCHARD STREET, W

tn It

/ x /

1905

FOREWORD

By Sir Joseph Walton, Knt.

Some books are valuable for what they teach us and others we prize for what they are. William Roper's book about Sir Thomas More may justly claim a place amongst the select few which are no less rich in matter than pleasing in form. In a style which may seem involved sometimes, but has nevertheless all the charm that belongs to our language in the vigour of its literary youth, he tells a story of the deepest human interest, and he tells of things which he himself had seen and heard, and remembered.

No figure which passes across the stage of English history has a more fascinating interest than that of Thomas More ; especially to those of us who profess the ancient faith for which he died, and now revere him as Blessed. And his life is something more than interesting. It appears to have been set up as an example and guide to those who from his time onward were to find their way through the difficulties of these latter days of intellectual enterprise and self-confidence, and of religious unrest.

In considering the true significance of the life and death of More it is well to recall the circumstances of the time in which he lived. The condition of the Church at the beginning of the 16th century has been much misrepresented, and there has been gross exaggeration of the abuses in its religious life and government. But what we ought to remember for our present purpose is (in the words of one of the most learned of living Catholic historians *) that "it may be admitted that the Church in life and discipline was not all that could be desired" and "that in many things there was need of reform in its truest sense."

This was appreciated by no one more truly or justly or with a keener insight than by Sir Thomas More. His delightful and never-failing sense of humour must not be forgotten. And we know that the pupil of Linacre and Grocyn, the close friend of Erasmus, the hospitable patron of Holbein rejoiced in all that was good and true and beautiful in the Renaissance of art and learning. But he gave up all—and life to him offered every attraction—and went cheerfully to death rather than be in any way a party to the revolt against the spiritual supremacy of the Pope.

This is the story which William Roper has to tell.

* Abbot Gasquet

Has it not, if we think of it, many lessons for all of us, whether we be of those whose impulse it is to look with confidence, and sometimes perhaps with too little patience, to the future, or of those whose nature it is to cling piously to the past and to resist perhaps even that inevitable movement by which the old order is ever changing giving place to the new? Sir Thomas More teaches us always, and in all events, patience and good temper and at the same time the strictest and most perfect loyalty to faith and conscience.

PREFACE

The First Edition

The Mirrour of Vertue in Worldly Greatnes, or *The Life of Sir Thomas More, Knight, sometime Lord Chancellor of England*, was first imprinted in the year 1626, at Paris, according to the title-page, though it has been suggested, without any definite proof, that the book was not really printed abroad.

The author of the Life, William Roper, Sir Thomas More's son-in-law, died in 1578 ; he had possibly not completed his book at the end of Queen Mary's reign. It is noteworthy that in 1557 Sir Thomas More's English works were first collected together and published, at the Queen's command, under the editorship of More's nephew, Justice Rastell, the elder son of the printer, John Rastell. In 1555 and 1556 the Latin works were published at Louvain. William Roper's precious memoir, described as *A Brief History of the Life, Arraignment, and Death of that Mirrour of all True Honour and Vertue, Syr Thomas More*, must have circulated in MS. for well-nigh seventy years, until at length " T. P." gave it to the press. Unfortunately the text he found was very faulty. " T. P." has not yet been identified, but may be Thomas Plowden. It is an interesting coincidence that a writer with the same initials, Thomas Paynell, the learned translator, added a table of contents to the afore-mentioned edition of More's English works. But this Thomas Paynell died in 1567, and " T. P." was the contemporary of Lady Elizabeth, Countess of Banbury, the second wife of William Knollys, upon whom Charles I conferred the Earldom of Banbury in August, 1626.

Other Biographies

Before the Life appeared in print the MS. version had already been utilised by various biographers of Sir Thomas More, notably by Stapleton, whose *Tres Thomæ* appeared at Antwerp in 1588 ; by Nicholas Harpsfield, whose work is preserved in Harleian MS. 6253 ; and by Cresacre

More, his great-grandson, whose *Life and Death of Sir Thomas More*, long erroneously assigned to his brother Thomas, was published without date or place, with a dedication to Queen Henrietta Maria ; it was probably printed in Paris or Louvain in 1631. Besides these there are other sixteenth-century *Lives of More* in MS. One of these, written in 1599, is printed in Wordsworth's *Ecclesiastical Biography*.

Editions of Roper's Life

Thomas Hearne, the famous antiquary, reprinted William Roper's book in the year 1716, but his text is almost as faulty as that of the *editio princeps*, though he had better MS. materials at his disposal ; he added various readings and emendations at the end of his volume. In 1729 the Rev. John Lewis, the biographer of Wiclif and Caxton, edited the Life from a fairly good MS. lent him by Mr. Thomas Beake, of Stourmouth, in Kent. In 1817 a new edition appeared, based on those of Hearne and Lewis, edited by S. W. Singer, the editor of Shakespeare. A much improved text was issued by him in 1822, amended by the collation of two MS. copies, both of these, according to his statement, in the handwriting of Roper's age, one of them belonging to Sir William

Strickland, Bart., of Boynton, in Yorkshire. It is an interesting fact that an earlier kinsman of the same name married one of the last female descendants of Margaret, Roper's wife.

The Present Edition

For the present issue Singer's modernised text has been utilised ; here and there some slight changes, notably in punctuation, have been made. Probably now, for the first time, More's verses, written with a coal after Master Secretary's visit to him in the Tower, are correctly given. In the four MS. copies of Roper's Life in the British Museum, namely, Harleian MSS. 6166, 6254, 6362, 7030, and in the printed copies, the versions of the lines make little sense. In Rastell's edition of *More's English Works* they are more correctly printed under the title of " Lewys, the Lost Lover." Together with the record left us by Sir Thomas More's son-in-law the biographical letters of his friend Erasmus should be read by way of commentary, and also More's own letters, more especially those to his favourite daughter Meg, and those from her to him : these famous letters between father and daughter are fittingly included in this volume.

Holbein's Portraits

To these literary documents should be added the portraits of More and his family, by his friend Hans Holbein, who came to England in 1526, possibly as More's guest at Chelsea, where he stayed about two years. The famous drawing among the Holbein treasures in the Royal Library at Windsor Castle, the basis of the engraving on the title-page of this volume, may be safely assigned to the year 1527.

"Thy painter," wrote More to Erasmus, who had introduced him, "is a wonderful artist, but I fear he will not find England as productive as he hopes, although I will do my best, as far as I am concerned, that he should not find it altogether barren." Holbein's sketch for his great picture of the family was seen by Erasmus in 1529. "Methought I saw shining through this beautiful household a soul even more beautiful." The artist had meanwhile returned to Basel, where what is generally thought to be the most authentic sketch is still preserved. There are three similar sketches, copies varying in details, in the possession of English families. The finished picture, if it ever existed, cannot be traced.

The life-story of Sir Thomas More has been a fruitful source of literary inspiration for prose, verse, and drama, from 1556, when Ellis Heywood wrote, in Florence, his dialogue *Il Moro*—a fanciful picture of More's relationship with the learned men of his time to the present day. Among modern tributes nothing exceeds in charm Miss Manning's *Household of Sir Thomas More*, the imaginary (though not altogether fictitious) diary of the noblest and most heroic of daughters, deservedly immortalised among " Fair Women."

> " Morn broadened on the borders of the dark
> Ere I saw her, who clasped in her last trance
> Her murdered father's head."

LIST OF CONTENTS

PAGE

TO THE RIGHT HONOURABLE
THE
LADY ELIZABETH COUNTESS
OF BANBURY, &c.

R<small>IGHT</small> H<small>ONOURABLE</small>,

It was my good happe not longe since, in a Friends House, to light upon a briefe History of the Life, Arraignement, and Death of that Mirrour of all true Honour, and Vertue, Syr Thomas More, who by his Wisdome, Learning, and Santity, hath eternized his Name, Countrey, and Profession, throughout the Christian World, with immortal Glory, and Renowne.

Finding, by perusal thereof, the same replenished with incomparable Treasures, of no lesse Worthy, and most Christian Factes, then of Wise, and Religious Sentences Apophthegmes, and Sayings; I deemed it not only an errour to permit so great a light to ly buried, as it were, within the walls of one priuate Family : but also iudged it worthy the Presse, euen of a golden Character (if it were to be had) to the end, the whole World might receaue comfort and profit by reading the same.

Having made this Resolution, a Difficultie presented itselfe, to my Thoughts, under whose Shadow, or Patronage I might best shelter the Worke : unto which strife, Your LADISHIP occurring to my cogitations, put an End, with the BEAMS of your WORTH, AND HONOUR ; so dazeling my Eyes, as I could discerne none other more Fit, or Worthy to imbrace, and protect so Glorious and memorable Example.

Of whose GOODNES I am so confident that without further debate, I judge, this Enterchange of Freendshippe may worthily be made betweene the SAINT and YOU. YOU (Madame) shal Patronize his HONOUR heere on Earth ; and He shall become a Patrone and Intercessour for YOU in Heaven.

By him, that am your Ladiships
professed Seruant,

T. P.

FORASMUCH as Sir Thomas More, Knight, sometime Lord Chancellor of England, a man of singular virtue and of a clear unspotted conscience (as witnesseth Erasmus), more pure and white than the whitest snow, and of such an angelical wit, as England, he saith, never had the like before, nor ever shall again : universally, as well in the laws of the realm (a study in effect able to occupy the whole life of a man) as in all other sciences, right well studied, was in his days accounted a man worthy perpetual famous memory—I, William Roper (though most unworthy), his son-in-law by marriage of his eldest daughter, knowing no one man that of him and of his doings understood so much as myself—for that I was continually resident in his house by the space of sixteen years and more—thought it therefore my part to set forth such matters touching his life as I could at this present call to remembrance, among which things very many notable, not meet to have been forgotten, through negligence and long con-

3

tinuance of time are slipped out of my mind. Yet to the intent that the same should not all utterly perish, I have— at the desire of divers worshipful friends of mine, though very far from the grace and worthiness of him, nevertheless, as far forth as my mean wit, memory and knowledge would serve me—declared so much thereof as in my poor judgment seemed worthy to be remembered.

THIS Sir Thomas More after he had been brought up in the Latin tongue at St. Anthony's in London, was by his father's procurement received into the house of the right reverend, wise and learned prelate Cardinal Morton, where though he was young of years, yet would he at Christmastide suddenly sometimes step in among the players, and never studying for the matter make a part of his own there presently among them, which made the lookers on more sport than all the players beside. In whose wit and towardness the Cardinal much delighting, would often say of him unto the nobles that divers times dined with him, "This child here waiting at the table, whosoever shall live to see it, will prove a marvellous man." Whereupon for his better furtherance in learning he placed him at Oxford, where when he was both in the Greek and Latin tongues sufficiently instructed, he was then, for the study of the law of the Realm, put

5

to an Inn of Chancery, called New Inn : where for his time he very well prospered, and from thence was admitted to Lincoln's Inn, with very small allowance, continuing there his study until he was made and accounted a worthy utter Barrister. After this, to his great commendations, he read for a good space a public lecture of St. Augustine *De Civitate Dei* in the church of St. Lawrence in the old Jewry, whereunto there resorted Doctor Grocyn, an excellent cunning man, and all the chief learned of the city of London. Then was he made reader of Furnival's Inn, so remaining by the space of three years and more. After which time he gave himself to devotion and prayer in the Charterhouse of London, religiously living there without vow about four years, until he resorted to the house of one Master Colte, a gentleman of Essex, that had oft invited him thither, having three daughters whose honest conversation and virtuous education provoked him there specially to set his affection. And albeit his mind most served him to the second daughter, for that he thought her the fairest and best favoured, yet when he considered that it would be both great grief and some shame also to the eldest to see her younger sister preferred before her in marriage, he then, of a certain pity, framed his fancy toward her, and soon

6

after married her, never the more discontinuing his study of the law at Lincoln's Inn, but applying still the same until he was called to the Bench, and had read there twice, which is as often as any Judge of the law doth ordinarily read. Before which time he had placed himself and his wife at Bucklersbury in London, where he had by her three daughters and one son, in virtue and learning brought up from their youth, whom he would often exhort to take virtue and learning for their meat, and play for their sauce. Who, ere ever he had been reader in Court, was in the latter time of King Henry the Seventh made a Burgess of the Parliament, wherein was demanded by the king (as I have heard reported) about three fifteenths for the marriage of his eldest daughter, that then should be the Scottish Queen. At the last debating whereof he made such arguments and reasons there against, that the king's demands were thereby clean overthrown ; so that one of the king's privy chamber, named Master Tyler, being present thereat, brought word to the king out of the Parliament house, that a beardless boy had disappointed all his purpose. Whereupon the king, conceiving great indignation towards him, could not be satisfied until he had some way revenged it. And forasmuch as he nothing having, nothing could lose, his grace devised

7

a causeless quarrel against his father, keeping him in the Tower till he had made him pay to him a hundred pounds fine. Shortly hereupon it fortuned that this Sir Thomas More coming in a suit to Doctor Fox, Bishop of Winchester, one of the king's privy council, the bishop called him aside, and pretending great favour towards him, promised that if he would be ruled by him, he would not fail into the king's favour again to restore him, meaning, as it was afterwards conjectured, to cause him thereby to confess his offence against the king, whereby his highness might with the better colour have occasion to revenge his displeasure against him. But when he came from the bishop, he fell in communication with one Master Whitforde, his familiar friend, then chaplain to that bishop, and afterward a father of Sion, and showed him what the bishop had said to him, desiring to have his advice therein ; who, for the passion of God, prayed him in no wise to follow his counsel, for "my lord, my master," quoth he, "to serve the king's turn will not stick to agree to his own father's death." So Sir Thomas More returned to the bishop no more, and had not the king soon after died, he was determined to have gone over sea, thinking that being in the king's indignation he could not live in England without great danger. After this he was made one of the under-sheriffs of London, by which office and his learning together (as I have heard him say) he gained without grief not so little as four hundred pounds by the year : sith there was at that time in none of the prince's courts of the laws of this realm any matter of importance in controversy wherein he was not with the one party of counsel. Of whom, for his learning, wisdom, knowledge and experience, men had such estimation, that before he came into the service of King Henry the Eighth, at the suit and instance of the English merchants, he was, by the king's consent, made twice ambassador in certain great causes between them and the merchants of the Stilliard. Whose wise and discreet dealing therein, to his high commendation, coming to the king's understanding, provoked his highness to cause Cardinal Wolsey, then Lord Chancellor, to procure him to his service. And albeit the cardinal, according to the king's request, earnestly travailed with him therefore, among many other his persuasions alleging unto him, how dear his service must needs be unto his majesty, which could not with his honour with less than he should yearly lose thereby, seem to recompense him. Yet he, loath to change his estate, made such means unto the king, by the cardinal, to the contrary, that his grace for

9

that time was well satisfied. Now happened there, after this, a great ship of his, that was then Pope, to arrive at Southampton, which the king claiming for a forfeiture, the Pope's ambassador, by suit unto his grace, obtained that he might for his master the Pope have counsel learned in the laws of this realm ; and the matter in his own presence (being himself a singular civilian), in some public place to be openly heard and discussed. At which time there could none of our law be found so meet to be of counsel with this ambassador as Sir Thomas More, who could report to the ambassador in Latin all the reasons and arguments by the learned counsel on both sides alleged. Upon this the counsellors on either part, in presence of the Lord Chancellor and other the judges in the Star Chamber had audience accordingly. Where Sir Thomas More not only declared to the ambassador the whole effect of all their opinions, but also in defence on the Pope's side argued so learnedly himself, that both was the aforesaid forfeiture restored to the Pope, and himself, among all the hearers, for his upright and commendable demeanour therein, so greatly renowned, that for no entreaty would the king from henceforth be induced any longer to forbear his service. At whose first entry thereunto he made him Master of the Requests, having then no better room void, and, within a month after, Knight, and one of his privy council. ∫ And so from time to time was he by the king advanced, continuing in his singular favour and trusty service twenty years and above. ∕A good part thereof used the king upon holy days when he had done his own devotions, to send for him into his traverse, and there— sometimes in matters of astronomy, geometry, divinity, and such other faculties, and sometimes of his worldly affairs—to sit and confer with him. And otherwhiles, in the night would he have him up into the leads, there to consider with him the diversities, courses, motions, and operations of the stars and planets. ∕ And because he was of a pleasant disposition, it pleased the king and queen, after the council had supped, at the time of their supper, for their pleasure commonly to call for him to be merry with them.˙ When he per-ceived them so much in his talk to delight, that he could not once in a month get leave to go home to his wife and his children (whose company he most desired), and to be absent from the court two days together but that he should be thither sent for again : he much misliking this restraint of his liberty, began thereupon somewhat to dissemble his nature, and so, by little and little, from his former mirth to disuse himself, that he was of them from henceforth at such

seasons no more so ordinarily sent for.| Then died
one Master Weston treasurer of the Exchequer, whose
office, after his death, the king of his own offer,
without any asking, freely gave unto Sir Thomas
More. In the fourteenth year of his grace's reign
there was a parliament holden, whereof Sir Thomas
More was chosen speaker. Who, being very loth to
take this room upon him, made an oration, not now
extant, to the king's highness, for his discharge thereof. Whereunto when the king would not consent,
he spoke unto his grace in form following :—

.

SITH, I perceive, most redoubted sovereign, that it standeth not with your pleasure to reform this election, and cause it to be changed, but have, by the mouth of the most reverend Father in God, the Legate, your highness' Chancellor, thereunto given your most royal assent, and have of your benignity determined, far above that I may bear, to enable me, and for this office to repute me meet ; rather than you should seem to impute unto your Commons, that they had unmeetly chosen : I am therefor, and always shall be ready, obediently to conform myself to the accomplishment of your highness' pleasure and commandment, in most humble wise beseeching your most noble Majesty, that I may, with your grace's favour, before I farther enter there into, make my humble intercession unto your highness for two lowly petitions : the one privately concerning myself, the other the whole assembly of your Commons' House. For myself, most gracious sovereign, that if it mishap

13

me in anything hereafter that is on the behalf of
your Commons, in your high presence to be declared,
to mistake my message, and in lack of good utterance,
by my mis-rehearsal, to pervert or impair their prudent instructions, that it may then like your most
noble majesty, of your abundant grace, with the eye
of your wonted pity to pardon my simpleness, giving
me leave to repair again unto the Commons' House,
and there to confer with them, and to take their substantial advice what things and in what wise I shall
on their behalf utter and speak before your noble
grace, to the intent their prudent devices and affairs
be not by my simpleness and folly hindered or impaired. Which thing, if it should so happen, as it
were well likely to mishap in me, if your grace's
benignity relieved not my oversight, it could not fail
to be during my life a perpetual grudge and heaviness
to my heart. The help and remedy whereof in
manner aforesaid remembered, is (most gracious
sovereign) my first lowly suit and humble petition
unto your noble grace. Mine other humble request,
most excellent prince, is this. Forasmuch as there
be of your Commons, here by your high commandment assembled for your parliament, a great number,
which are after the accustomed manner appointed,
in the Commons' House to treat and advise of the

common affairs among themselves apart : and albeit, most dear liege lord, that according to your prudent advice, by your honourable writs everywhere declared, there hath been as due diligence used in sending up to your highness' Court of Parliament the most discreet persons out of every quarter that men could esteem meet thereto. Whereby it is not to be doubted but that there is a very substantial assembly of right wise meet and politique persons. Yet, most victorious prince, sith, among so many wise men, neither is every man wise alike, nor, among so many men alike well witted, every man alike well spoken, and it often happeth that likewise as much folly is uttered with painted polished speech, so, many, boisterous and rude in language, see deep indeed, and give right substantial counsel ; and sith also in matters of great importance the mind is so often occupied in the matter, that a man rather studieth what to say, than how ; by reason whereof the wisest man and best spoken in a whole country fortuneth while his mind is fervent in the matter, somewhat to speak in such wise as he would afterward wish to have been uttered otherwise, and yet no worse will had he when he spake it, than he hath when he would so gladly change it. Therefore, most gracious sovereign, considering that, in all your high Court of Parliament, is nothing treated but matter of weight and importance concerning your realm and your own royal estate, it could not fail to let and put to silence from the giving of their advice and counsel many of your discreet Commons, to the great hindrance of the common affairs, except that every one of your Commons were utterly discharged of all doubt and fear how any thing, that it should happen them to speak, should happen of your highness to be taken. And in this point, though your well known and proved benignity putteth every man in good hope, yet such is the weight of the matter, such is the reverend dread that the timorous hearts of your natural subjects conceive towards your highness, our most redoubted king and undoubted sovereign, that they cannot, in this point, find themselves satisfied, except your gracious bounty therein declared put away the scruple of their timorous minds, and animate and encourage them and put them out of doubt. It may therefore like your most abundant grace, our most benign and godly king, to give to all your Commons, here assembled, your most gracious license and pardon, freely, without doubt of your dreadful displeasure, every man to discharge his conscience, and boldly, in every thing incident among us, to declare his advice ; and, whatsoever happeneth any man to say, that it

16

may like your noble majesty of your inestimable goodness to take all in good part, interpreting every man's words, how uncunningly soever they be couched, to proceed yet of good zeal towards the profit of your realm and honour of your royal person, the prosperous estate and perservation whereof, most excellent sovereign, is the thing which we all, your humble loving subjects, according to the most bounden duty of our natural allegiance, most highly desire and pray for.

AT this Parliament Cardinal Wolsey found him-self much grieved with the burgesses thereof, for that nothing was so soon done or spoken therein but that it was immediately blown abroad in every alehouse. It fortuned at that Parliament a very great subsidy to be demanded, which the Cardinal fearing would not pass the Commons' House deter-mined for the furtherance thereof to be there present himself. Before whose coming, after long debating there, whether it were better but with a few of his lords, as the most opinion of the house was, or with his whole train royally, to receive him there amongst them : " Masters," quoth Sir Thomas More, " foras-much as my Lord Cardinal lately, ye wot well, laid to our charge the lightness of our tongues for things uttered out of this house, it shall not in my mind be amiss to receive him with all his pomp, with his maces, his pillars, his poleaxes, his crosses, his hat and the great seal too ; to the intent that if he find the like fault with us hereafter, we may be the bolder from ourselves to lay the blame on those that his grace bringeth hither with him." Whereunto the house wholly agreeing, he was received accordingly. Where after he had in a solemn oration by many reasons proved how necessary it was the demand there moved to be granted, and further showed that less would not serve to maintain the prince's purpose, he seeing the company sitting still silent and thereunto nothing answering, and contrary to his expectations showing in themselves towards his request no towardness of inclination, said unto them, " Masters, you have many wise and learned men amongst you, and sith I am from the king's own person sent hither unto you for the preservation of yourselves and all the realm, I think it meet you give me some reasonable answer." Whereat every man holding his peace, then began he to speak to one Master Marney, afterward Lord Marney, " How say you," quoth he, " Master Marney ? " who making him no answer neither, he severally asked the same question of divers others accounted the wisest of the company : to whom, when none of them all would give so much as one word, being agreed before, as the custom was, to answer by their Speaker, " Masters," quoth the Cardinal, " unless it be the manner of your house, as of likelihood it is, by the mouth of your Speaker, whom you have chosen for trusty and wise (as indeed he is), in such cases to utter your minds, here is without doubt a marvellous obstinate silence," and thereupon he required answer of Master Speaker. Who first reverently on his knees excusing the silence of the house, abashed at the presence of so noble a personage, able to amaze the wisest and best learned in the realm, and after by many probable arguments proving that for them to make answer was neither expedient nor agreeable with the ancient liberty of the house ; in conclusion for himself showed that though they had all with their voices trusted him, yet except every one of them could put into his one head all their several wits, he alone in so weighty a matter was unmeet to make his grace answer. Whereupon the cardinal, displeased with Sir Thomas More, that had not in this parliament in all things satisfied his desire, suddenly arose and departed. And after the parliament ended, in his gallery at Whitehall in Westminster, he uttered unto him all his griefs, saying : "Would to God you had been at Rome, Master More, when I made you Speaker." "Your grace not offended, so would I too, my lord," quoth Sir Thomas More. And to wind such quarrels out of the cardinal's head, he began to talk of the gallery, saying, "I like this gallery of yours, my lord, much better than your gallery at Hampton Court." Wherewith so wisely broke he off the cardinal's displeasant talk, that the cardinal at that present, as it seemed, wist not what more say to him ; but, for the revengement of his displeasure, counselled the king to send him ambassador to Spain, commending to his highness his wisdom, learning and meetness for that voyage. And, the difficulty of the cause considered, none was there, he said, so well able to serve his grace therein. Which when the king had broken to Sir Thomas More, and that he had declared unto his grace how unfit a journey it was for him, the nature of the country, the disposition of his complexion so disagreeing together, that he should never be able to do his grace acceptable service there, knowing right well that if his grace sent him thither he should send him to his grave ; but showing himself nevertheless ready according to his duty, or were it with the loss of his life, to fulfill his grace's pleasure in that behalf. The king, allowing well his answer, said unto him : "It is not our pleasure, Master More, to do you hurt, but to do you good we would be glad : we therefore for this purpose will devise upon some other, and employ your service otherwise." And such entire favour did the king bear him, that he made him Chancellor of the Duchy of Lancaster upon the death of Sir Richard Wingfield who had that office before. And for the pleasure he took in his company would his grace suddenly sometimes come home to his house at Chelsea to be merry with him, whither, on a time, unlooked for, he came to dinner, and after dinner, in a fair garden of his, walked with him by the space of an hour, holding his arm about his neck. As soon as his grace was gone, I rejoicing thereat, said to Sir Thomas More, how happy he was whom the king had so familiarly entertained, as I never had seen him do to any before, except Cardinal Wolsey, whom I saw his grace walk once with arm in arm. "I thank our Lord, son," quoth he, "I find his grace my very good lord indeed, and I believe he doth as singularly favour me, as any subject within this realm : howbeit, son Roper, I may tell thee, I have no cause to be proud thereof, for if my head would win him a castle in France (for then there was war between us), it should not fail to go."

THIS Sir Thomas More, among all other his virtues, was of such meekness, that if it had fortuned him with any learned men resorting to him from Oxford, Cambridge, or elsewhere (as there did divers, some for desire of his acquaintance, some for the famous report of his wisdom and learning, some for suits of the Universities), to have entered into argument (wherein few were comparable to him) and so far to have discoursed with them therein, that he might perceive they could not without some inconvenience hold out much further disputation against him ; then, lest he should discomfort them (as one that sought not his own glory, but rather would seem conquered than to discourage students in their studies, ever showing himself more desirous to learn than to teach), would he by some witty device courteously break off into some other matter and give over.   Of whom, for his wisdom and learning, had the king such an opinion, that at such time as he attended upon his highness, taking his progress either to Oxford or Cambridge, where he was received with very eloquent orations, his grace would always assign him (as one that was most prompt and ready therein) extempore to make answer thereunto. Whose manner was, whensoever he had occasion, either here or beyond the sea, to be in any University, not only to be present at the readings and disputations there commonly used, but also learnedly to dispute among them himself. Who being chancellor of the duchy was made ambassador twice, joined in commission with Cardinal Wolsey ; once to the Emperor Charles into Flanders, the other time to the French king into France. Not long after this, the Water-bailiff of London, sometime his servant, hearing, where he had been at dinner, certain merchants liberally to rail against his old master, waxed so discontented therewith that he hastily came to him and told him what he had heard, "and were I, Sir," quoth he, "in such favour and authority with my prince as you are, such men surely should not be suffered so villainously and falsely to misreport and slander me. Wherefore I would wish you to call them before you, and, to their shame, for their lewd malice to punish them." Who, smiling upon him said, "why, Master Water-bailiff, would you have me punish them by whom I receive more benefit than by all you that be my friends ? Let them a God's name speak as lewdly as they list of me, and shoot never so many arrows at me as long as they do not hit me, what am I the worse ? But if they should once hit me, then would it indeed not a little trouble me ; howbeit I trust by God's help there shall none of them all once be able to touch me. I have more cause, I assure thee, Master Water-bailiff, to pity them than to be angry with them." Such fruitful communication had he ofttimes with his familiar friends. So on a time walking with me along the Thames' side at Chelsea, in talking of other things he said unto me, "Now, would to our Lord, son Roper, upon condition that three things were well established in Christendom, I were put in a sack and here presently cast into the Thames." "What great things be those, Sir," quoth I, "that should move you so to wish ?" "Wouldst thou know, son Roper, what they be," quoth he ? "Yea marry with a good will, Sir, if it please you," quoth I. "In faith, son, they be these," said he, "the first is, that whereas the most part of Christian princes be at mortal war, they were all at universal peace. The second, that where the church of Christ is at this present sore afflicted with many errors and heresies, it were well settled in perfect uniformity of religion. The third, that where the matter of the king's marriage is now come in question, it were to the glory of God and quietness of all parties brought to a good conclusion." Whereby as I could gather, he judged that otherwise it would be a disturbance to a great part of Christendom. Thus did it, by his doings throughout the whole course of his life, appear, that all his travail and pains, without respect of earthly commodities, either to himself, or any of his, were only upon the service of God, the prince, and the realm, wholly bestowed and employed ; whom I heard in his latter time to say that he never asked of the king for himself the value of one penny.

AS Sir Thomas More's custom was daily (if he were at home), besides his private prayers with his children, to say the Seven Psalms, the Litany, and the Suffrages following, so was his guise nightly before he went to bed with his wife, children, and household, to go to his chapel, and there on his knees ordinarily to say certain psalms and collects with them. And because he was desirous for godly purposes, sometimes to be solitary and sequester himself from worldly company, a good distance from his mansion-house, builded he a place called the New Building, wherein there was a chapel, a library, and a gallery, in which, as his use was on other days to occupy himself in prayer and study there together, so on the Fridays used he continually to be there from morning till evening, spending his time only in devout prayers and spiritual exercises. And to provoke his wife and children to the desire of heavenly things, he would sometimes use these words unto them. "It is now no mastery for you children to go to heaven, for every body giveth you good counsel, every body giveth you good example. You see virtue rewarded and vice punished, so that you are carried up to heaven even by the chins. But if you live in the time that no man will give you good counsel, no man will give you good example, when you shall see virtue punished and vice rewarded, if you will then stand fast and firmly stick to God upon pain of life, though you be but half good, God will allow you for whole good." If his wife or any of his children had been diseased or troubled, he would say unto them, "may not look at our pleasures to go to heaven in featherbeds ; it is not the way, for our Lord Himself went thither with great pain, and by many tribulations, which was the path wherein He walked thither, and the servant may not look to be in better case than his Master."⌉ And as he would in this sort persuade them to take their troubles patiently, so would he in like sort teach them to withstand the devil and his temptations valiantly, saying, "whosoever will mark the devil and his temptations shall find him therein much like to an ape, who, not well looked to, will be busy and bold to do shrewd turns, and contrariwise being spied will suddenly leap back and adventure no farther. So the devil finding a man idle, slothful, and without resistance, ready to receive his temptations, waxeth so hardy that he will not fail still to continue with him until to his purpose he hath thoroughly brought him. But on the other side, if he see a man with diligence persevere to prevent and withstand his temptations, he waxeth so weary that in conclusion he utterly forsaketh him. For as the devil of disposition is a spirit of so high a pride that he cannot abide to be mocked, so is he of nature so envious that he feareth any more to assault him, lest he should thereby not only catch a foul fall himself, but also minister to the man more matter of merit." Thus delighted he evermore not only in virtuous exercises to be occupied by himself, but also to exhort his wife, children, and household to embrace the same and follow it. To whom for his notable virtue and godliness God showed as it seemed a manifest miraculous token of His special favour towards him. At such time as my wife (as many other that year were) was sick of the sweating sickness ; who lying in so great extremity of that disease as by no invention or devices that physicians in such cases commonly use (of whom she had divers both expert, wise, and well learned, then continually attendant about her) could she be kept from sleep, so that both the physicians and all other there present despaired of her recovery and gave her over ; her father, as he that most entirely tendered her, being in no small heaviness for her, by prayer at God's hand sought to get her remedy. Whereupon going up, after his usual manner, into his aforesaid New Building there in his chapel on his knees with tears most devoutly besought Almighty God that it would like His goodness, unto whom nothing was impossible, if it were His blessed will, at his mediation, to vouch-safe graciously to hear his humble petition. Where incontinent came into his mind that a glister should be the only way to help her. Which when he told the physicians, they by and by confessed that if there were any hope of health that that was the very best help indeed ; much marvelling of themselves that they had not before remembered it. Then was it immediately administered to her sleeping, which she could by no means have been brought unto waking. And albeit, after she was thereby thoroughly awaked, God's marks (an evident undoubted token of death) plainly appeared upon her, yet she, contrary to all their expectations, was, as it was thought, by her father's most fervent prayers miraculously recovered, and at length again to perfect health restored ; whom, if it had pleased God at that time to have taken to His mercy, her father said he would never have meddled with worldly matters more.

NOW while Sir Thomas More was chancellor of the duchy, the see of Rome chanced to be void, which was cause of much trouble. For Cardinal Wolsey, a man very ambitious, and desirous (as good hope and likelihood he had) to aspire to that dignity, perceiving himself of his expectation disappointed, by means of the Emperor Charles so highly commending one Cardinal Adrian, sometime his schoolmaster, to the cardinals of Rome in the time of their election for his virtue and worthiness, that thereupon he was chosen pope ; who from Spain, where he was then resident, coming on foot to Rome before his entry into the city did put off his hose and shoes, and barefooted and barelegged passed through the streets towards his palace with such humbleness that all the people had him in great reverence ; Cardinal Wolsey, I say, waxed so wood therewith, that he studied to invent all ways of revengement of his grief against the emperor ; which as it was the beginning of a lamentable tragedy, so some part thereof, as not impertinent to my present purpose, I reckoned requisite here to put in remembrance. This cardinal therefore, not ignorant of the king's inconstant and mutable disposition, soon inclined to withdraw his devotion from his most noble, virtuous, and lawful wife Queen Katherine, aunt to the emperor, upon every light occasion ; and upon other, to her in nobility, wisdom, virtue, favour, and beauty far incomparable, to fix his affection : meaning to make this his so light disposition an instrument to bring about his ungodly intent, devised to allure the king (then already contrary to his mind nothing less looking for than falling in love with the Lady Anne Bullen) to cast fantasy unto one of the French king's sisters. Which thing (because of the enmity and war that was at that time between the French king and the emperor, whom, for the cause before remembered, he mortally maligned) he was very desirous to procure. And for the better achieving thereof requested Longland, Bishop of Lincoln, being ghostly father to the king, to put a scruple into his grace's head, that it was not lawful for him to marry his brother's wife. Which the king not sorry to hear of, opened it first to Sir Thomas More, whose counsel he required therein, showing him certain places of Scripture that seemed somewhat to serve his appetite. Which when he had perused, and thereupon, as one that never had professed the study of divinity, himself excused to be unmeet many ways to meddle with such matters, the king, not satisfied with his answer, so sore still pressed upon him therefore, that in conclusion he condescended to his grace's motion. And farther, forasmuch as the case was of such importance as needed good advisement and deliberation, he besought his grace of sufficient respite advisedly to consider of it. Wherewith the king, well contented, said unto him, that Tunstal and Clarke, Bishops of Bath and Durham, with other learned of his privy council, should also be dealers therein. So Sir Thomas More departing conferred those places of Scripture with the exposition of divers of the old holy doctors. And at his coming to the court in talking with his grace of the foresaid matter, he said, "To be plain with your grace, neither my Lord of Durham, nor my Lord of Bath, though I know them both to be wise, virtuous, learned and honourable prelates, nor myself with the rest of your council, being all your grace's own servants, for your manifold benefits daily bestowed on us so much bounden unto you, be in my judgment meet counsellors for your grace herein. But if your grace mind to understand the truth, such counsellors may you have devised, as neither for respect of their own worldly commodity, nor for fear of your princely authority, will be inclined to deceive you." To whom he named then St. Jerome, St. Augustine, and divers other old holy doctors both Greeks and Latins : and moreover showed him what authorities he had gathered out of them. Which although the king (as disagreeable to his desire) did not very well like of, yet were they by Sir Thomas More (who in all his communication with the king in that matter had always most discreetly behaved himself) so wisely tempered, that he both presently took them in good part, and oftentimes had thereof conference with him again. After this were there certain questions among his council proponed, Whether the king needed in this case to have any scruple at all ? and if he had, what way were best to be taken to deliver him of it ? The most part of them were of the opinion that there was good cause of scruple, and that for the discharging of it, suit were meet to be made to the see of Rome, where the king hoped by liberality to obtain his purpose ; wherein, as it after appeared, he was far deceived. Then was there, for the examination and trial of this matrimony, procured from Rome a commission in which Cardinal Campegius, and Cardinal Wolsey were joined commissioners, who for the determination thereof sat at the Black-Friars in London, where a libel was put in for the annulling of the said matrimony, alleging the marriage between the king and queen to be unlawful. And for proof of the marriage to be lawful was there brought in a dispensation, in which after divers disputations thereupon holden, there appeared an imperfection ; which, by an instrument or brief, found upon search in the treasury of Spain and sent to the commissioners in England, was supplied. And so should judgment have been given by the pope accordingly, had not the king, upon intelligence thereof, before the same judgment, appealed to the next general council ; after whose appellation the cardinals upon that matter sat no longer. It fortuned, before the matter of the said matrimony brought in question, when I in talk with Sir Thomas More (of a certain joy) commended unto him the happy estate of this realm, that had so catholic a prince that no heretic durst show his face ; so virtuous and learned a clergy, so grave and sound a nobility, and so loving obedient subjects all in one faith agreeing together. " Troth, it is indeed, son Roper," quoth he, (and went far beyond me in commending all degrees and estates of the same), " and yet, son Roper, I pray God," said he, " that some of us, as high as we seem to sit upon the mountains treading heretics under our feet like ants, live not the day that we gladly would wish to be at league and composition with them to let them have their churches quietly to themselves, so that they would be contented to let us have ours quietly to ourselves." After that I had told him many considerations why he had no cause to say so ; "Well," said he, "I pray God, son Roper, some of us live not till that day " : showing me no reason why I should put any doubt therein. To whom I said, " By my troth, sir, it is very desperately spoken." That vile term, I cry God mercy, did I give him : who, by these words perceiving me in a fume, said merrily unto me, "Well, well, son Roper, it shall not be so, it shall not be so." Whom in sixteen years and more, being in his house conversant with him, I could never perceive as much as once in a fume.

BUT now to return again where I left. After the supplying of the imperfection of the dispensation, sent, as is before rehearsed, to the commissioners into England, the king, taking the matter for ended, and then meaning no farther to proceed in that matter, appointed the Bishop of Durham and Sir Thomas More to go ambassadors to Cambray, a place neither Imperial nor French, to treat a peace between the Emperor, the French king, and him. In the concluding whereof Sir Thomas More so worthily handled himself, procuring in our league far more benefits unto this realm, than at that time by the king or his council was thought possible to be compassed, that for his good service in that voyage, the king, when he after made him Lord Chancellor, caused the Duke of Norfolk openly to declare to the people, as you shall hear hereafter more at large, how much all England was bounden unto him. Now upon the coming home of the Bishop of Durham and

Sir Thomas More from Cambray the king was as earnest of persuading Sir Thomas More to agree to the matter of his marriage as before, by many and divers ways provoking him thereunto, for which, as it was thought, he the rather soon after made him Lord Chancellor, and farther declaring unto him that though at his going over sea to Cambray he was in utter despair thereof, yet he had conceived since some good hope to compass it. For albeit his marriage, being against the positive laws of the church, and against the written law of God, was holpen by the dispensation, yet was there another thing found out of late, he said, whereby his marriage appeared to be so directly against the law of nature that it could in no wise by the church be dispensable, as Doctor Stokesley, whom he had then [newly] preferred to be Bishop of London, and in that case chiefly credited, was able to instruct him : with whom he prayed him in that point to confer. But for all his conference with him he saw nothing of such force as could induce him to change his opinion therein. Which notwith-standing, the bishop showed himself in his report of him to the king's highness so good and favourable, that he said he found him in his grace's cause very toward, and desirous to find some good matter where-with he might truly serve his grace to his contentation. This Bishop Stokesley, being by the cardinal not long before in the Star-chamber openly put to rebuke, and awarded to the Fleet, not brooking this contumelious usage, and thinking that forasmuch as the cardinal, for lack of such forwardness in setting forth the king's divorce as his grace looked for, was out of his highness' favour, he had now a good occasion offered him to revenge his quarrel; farther to increase the king's displeasure towards him, busily travailed to invent some colourable device for the king's furtherance in that behalf; which, as before is remembered, he to his grace revealed, hoping thereby to bring the king to the better liking of himself and the more misliking of the cardinal, whom his highness therefore soon after of his office displaced, and to Sir Thomas More, the rather to move him to incline to his side, the same in his stead committed. Who between the Dukes of Norfolk and Suffolk being brought through Westminster Hall to his place in the Chancery, the Duke of Norfolk, in audience of all the people there assembled, showed, that he was from the king himself straightly charged by special commission, there openly in presence of them all, to make declaration how much all England was beholden unto Sir Thomas More for his good service, and how worthy he was to have the highest room in the realm, and how dearly his grace loved and trusted him, for which, said the duke, he had great cause to rejoice. Whereunto Sir Thomas More, amongst many other his humble and wise sayings not now in my memory, answered, that although he had good cause to take comfort of his highness' singular favour towards him, that he had, far above his deserts, so highly commended him, to whom therefore he acknowledged himself most deeply bounden : yet nevertheless he must for his own part needs confess that in all things by his grace alleged he had done no more than was his duty : and farther disabled himself to be unmeet for that room, wherein, considering how wise and honourable a prelate had lately before taken so great a fall, he said he had no cause thereof to rejoice. And as they had charged him, on the king's behalf, uprightly to administer indifferent justice to the people, without corruption or affection, so did he likewise charge them again that if they saw him at any time in any thing digress from any part of his duty in that honourable office, even as they would discharge their own duty and fidelity to God and the king, so should they not fail to disclose it to his grace, who otherwise might have just occasion to lay his fault wholly to their charge.

WHILE he was Lord Chancellor, being at leisure (as seldom he was), one of his sons-in-law on a time said merrily unto him : "When Cardinal Wolsey was Lord Chancellor, not only divers of his privy chamber, but such also as were his doorkeepers, gat great gain"; (and since he had married one of his daughters, and gave still attendance upon him, he thought he might of reason look for some) ; where he indeed, because he was ready himself to hear every man, poor and rich, and keep no doors shut from them, could find none ; which was to him a great discouragement. And whereas some for friendship, some for kindred, and some for profit would gladly have his furtherance in bringing them to his presence, if he should now take any thing of them, he knew, he said, he should do them great wrong, for that they might do as much for themselves as he could do for them. Which condition, though he thought in Sir Thomas More very commendable, yet to him, he said, being his son he found it nothing profitable. When he had told him this tale, "you say well, son," quoth he, " I do not mislike that you are of conscience so scrupulous ; but many other ways be there, son, that I may both do you good, and pleasure your friend also. For sometime may I by my word stand your friend in stead, and sometime may I by my letter help him ; or if he have a cause depending before me, at your request I may hear him before another. Or if his cause be not all the best, yet may I move the parties to fall to some reasonable end by arbitrement. Howbeit this one thing, son, I assure thee on my faith, that if the parties will at my hands call for justice, then all-were-it my father stood on the one side, and the devil on the other, his cause being good, the devil should have right." So offered he his son as he thought, he said, so much favour as he could with reason require. And that he would for no respect digress frɔm justice, well appeared by a plain example of another of his sons-in-law called Master Heron. For when he, having a matter before him in the Chancery, and presuming too much of his favour, would by him in no wise be persuaded to agree to any indifferent order, then made he in conclusion a flat decree against him. This Lord Chancellor used commonly every afternoon to sit in his open hall, to the intent that if any person had any suit unto him, they might the more boldly come to his presence, and there open their complaints before him. Whose manner was also to read every bill himself, ere he would award any *subpœna*, which bearing matter worthy a *subpœna* would he set his hand unto, or else cancel it. Whensoever he passed through Westminster Hall to his place in the Chancery, by the Court of the King's Bench, if his father (one of the judges thereof) had been seated or he came, he would go into the same court, and there reverently kneeling down, in the sight of them all, duly ask his father's blessing. And if it fortuned that his father and he at readings in Lincoln's Inn met together, (as they sometimes did) notwithstanding his high office he would offer in argument the pre-eminence to his father, though he, for his office sake, would refuse to take it. And for the better declaration of his natural affection towards his father, he not only, while he lay in his death bed, according to his duty, oft-times with comfortable words most kindly came to visit him, but also at his departure out of the world, with tears taking him about the neck most lovingly kissed and embraced him, commending him into the merciful hands of Almighty God, and so departed from him. And as few in-

43

junctions as he granted while he was Lord Chancellor, yet were they by some of the judges of the law misliked; which I understanding declared the same unto Sir Thomas More. Who answered me that they should have little cause to find fault with him therefore, and thereupon caused he one Master Crooke, chief of the Six Clerks, to make a docket containing the whole number and causes of all such injunctions as either in his time had already passed, or at that present depended in any of the king's courts at Westminster before him. Which done he invited all the Judges to dine with him in the council chamber at Westminster; where, after dinner, when he had broken with them what complaints he had heard of his injunctions, and moreover showed them both the number and causes of every one of them, in order so plainly, that, upon full debating of those matters, they were all enforced to confess that they, in like case, could have done no otherwise themselves. Then offered he this unto them: that if the justices of every court unto whom the reformation of the rigour of the law, by reason of their office, most especially appertained, would upon reasonable considerations by their own discretions, as they were, as he thought, in conscience bound, mitigate and reform the rigour of the law themselves, there should from thenceforth by him no more injunctions be granted. Whereunto, when they refused to condescend, then said he unto them, " Forasmuch as yourselves, my lords, drive me to that necessity for awarding out injunctions to relieve the people's injury, you cannot hereafter any more justly blame me." After that he said secretly to me : " I perceive, son, why they like not so to do. For they see that they may, by the verdict of the jury, cast off all quarrels from themselves upon them, which they account their chief defence ; and therefore am I compelled to abide the adventure of all such reports." And, as little leisure as he had to be occupied in the study of the Holy Scripture, and controversies about religion, and such other virtuous exercises, being in a manner continually busied about the affairs of the king and the realm, yet such watch and pain in setting forth of divers profitable works in the defence of the true Christian religion, against heresies secretly sown abroad in the realm, assuredly sustained he, that the bishops (to whose pastoral care the reformation thereof most principally appertained) thinking themselves by his travail (wherein by their own confession they were not able with him to make comparison) of their duties in that behalf discharged ; and, considering that, for all his prince's favour, he was no rich man,

45

nor in yearly revenues advanced as his worthiness deserved ; therefore, at a convocation among themselves and others of the clergy, they agreed together and concluded upon a sum of four or five thousand pounds, at the least, to my remembrance, for his pains to recompense him. To the payment whereof every bishop, abbot, and the rest of the clergy were after the rate of their abilities liberal contributors, hoping that this portion should be to his contentation. Whereupon Tunstal, Bishop of Durham, Clarke, Bishop of Bath, and as far as I can call to mind, Vaysye, Bishop of Exeter, repaired unto him, declaring how thankfully for his travails to their discharge in God's cause bestowed, they reckoned themselves bounden to consider him. And that albeit they could not according to his desert, so worthily as they gladly would, requite him therefore, but must refer that only to the goodness of God ; yet for a small part of recompense in respect of his estate, so unequal to his worthiness, in the name of their whole convocation they presented unto him that sum, which they desired him to take in good part. Who, forsaking it, said, that like as it was no small comfort unto him that so wise and learned men so well accepted his simple doings, for which he never intended to receive reward but at the hands of God only, to whom alone was the thank thereof chiefly to be ascribed ; so gave he most humble thanks unto their honours all for their so bountiful and friendly consideration. When they, for all their importunate pressing upon him (that few would have weened he could have refused) could by no means make him to take it, then besought they him to be content yet that they might bestow it on his wife and children. "Not so, my lords," quoth he, " I had liever see it cast into the Thames, than either I or any of mine should have thereof the worth of a penny. For though your offer, my lords, be indeed very friendly and honourable, yet set I so much by my pleasure, and so little by my profit, that I would not, in good faith, have lost the rest of so many a night's sleep as was spent upon the same, for much more than your liberal offer. And yet wish would I for all that, upon condition that all heresies were suppressed, that all my books were burned, and my labour utterly lost." Thus departing were they fain to restore unto every man his own again.

THIS Lord Chancellor, albeit he was to God and the world well known to be of notable virtue, though not so of every man considered, yet, for the avoiding of singularity, would he appear no otherwise than other men in his apparel and other behaviour. And albeit he appeared outwardly honourable like one of his calling, yet inwardly he, no such vanities esteeming, secretly next his body wore a shirt of hair. Which my sister More, a young gentlewoman, in the summer as he sat at supper singly in his doublet and hose, wearing thereupon a plain shirt without either ruff or collar, chancing to espy, began to laugh at it. My wife, not ignorant of his manner, perceiving the same, privily told him of it, and he being sorry that she saw it, presently amended it. He also sometimes used to punish his body with whips, the cords knotted, which was known only to my wife, his eldest daughter, whom, for her secrecy, above all other he specially trusted, causing her, as need required, to wash the same shirt of hair. Now shortly upon his entry into the high office of the chancellorship, the king eftsoons again moved him to weigh and consider his great matter. Who falling down on his knees, humbly besought his highness to stand his gracious sovereign, as ever since his entry into his gracious service he had found him, saying, there was nothing in the world had been so grievous unto his heart, as to remember that he was not able (as he willingly would with the loss of one of his limbs), for that matter, anything to find whereby he could serve his grace to his contentation, as he that always bare in mind the most godly words that his highness spake unto him at his first coming into his noble service, the most virtuous lesson that ever prince taught his servant : willing him first to look unto God, and after God unto him : as in good faith, he said, he did, or else might his grace well account him his most unworthy servant. To this the king answered, that if he could not therein with his conscience serve him, he was content to accept his service otherwise, and, using the advice of other of his learned council whose consciences could well enough agree therewith, would nevertheless continue his gracious favour towards him, and never with that matter molest his conscience afterward. But Sir

Thomas More in process of time seeing the king fully determined to proceed forth in the marriage of Queen Anne : and when he with the bishops and nobles of the higher house of parliament were, for the furtherance of that marriage, commanded by the king to go down unto the Commons' House, to show unto them both what the Universities, as well of other parts beyond the seas as of Oxford and Cambridge, had done in that behalf, and their seals also testifying the same, all which matters, at the king's request, not showing of what mind himself was therein, he opened to the lower house of the parliament. Nevertheless, doubting lest further attempts after should follow, which, contrary to his conscience, by reason of his office, he was likely to be put unto, he made suit unto the Duke of Norfolk, his singular dear friend, to be a mean to the king that he might, with his grace's favour, be discharged of that chargeable room of the chancellorship, wherein, for certain infirmities of his body, he pretended himself unable any longer to serve. This duke, coming on a time to Chelsea to dine with him, fortuned to find him at the church, in the quire, with a surplice on his back, singing. To whom, after service, as they went homeward together arm in arm, the duke said, " God's body, God's body, my Lord Chancellor, a

parish clerk, a parish clerk! You dishonour the
king, and his office." "Nay," quoth Sir Thomas
More, smiling on the duke, "your grace may not
think that the king, your master and mine, will with
me for serving of God his master, be offended, or
thereby account his office dishonoured." When the
duke, being thereunto often solicited, by importunate
suit had at length of the king obtained for Sir
Thomas More a clear discharge of his office, then, at
a time convenient, by his highness' appointment,
repaired he to his grace to yield up to him the great
seal. Which, as his grace with thanks and praise for
his worthy service in that office, courteously at his
hands received, so pleased it his highness to say more
unto him ; that for the good service which he before
had done him, in any suit which he should after
have unto him, that should either concern his
honour—for that word it pleased his highness to use
unto him—or that should appertain unto his profit,
he should find his highness good and gracious lord
unto him. After he had thus given over the chancellorship, and placed all his gentlemen and yeomen
with noblemen and bishops, and his eight watermen
with the Lord Audley that in the same office succeeded
him, to whom also he gave his great barge : then
calling us all that were his children unto him, and

51

asking our advice how we might now in this decay of his ability, by the surrender of his office so impaired, that he could not as he was wont, and gladly would, bear out the whole charges of them all himself, from thenceforth be able to live and continue together, as he wished we should ; when he saw us silent, and in that case not ready to show our opinions unto him, "then will I," said he, "show my poor mind to you. I have been brought up," quoth he, "at Oxford, at an Inn of the Chancery, at Lincoln's Inn, and also in the king's court, and so forth from the lowest degree to the highest, and yet have I in yearly revenues at this present left me little above a hundred pounds by the year. So that now we must hereafter, if we like to live together, be contented to become contributaries together. But by my counsel it shall not be best for us to fall to the lowest fare first; we will not, therefore, descend to Oxford fare, nor to the fare of New Inn, but we will begin with Lincoln's Inn diet, where many right-worshipful and of good years do live full well. Which, if we find not ourselves the first year able to maintain, then we will the next year go one step down to New Inn fare, wherewith many an honest man is well contented. If that exceed our ability too, then will we, the next year after, descend to

Oxford fare, where many grave learned and ancient fathers be continually conversant. Which, if our ability stretch not to maintain neither ; then may we yet, with bags and wallets, go a-begging together, and hoping that for pity some good folk will give us their charity, at every man's door to sing *Salve Regina*, and so still keep company and be merry together." And whereas you have heard before, he was by the king from a very worshipful living taken into his grace's service, with whom, in all the great and weighty causes that concerned his highness or the realm, he consumed and spent with painful cares, travail, and trouble, as well beyond the seas as within the realm, in effect, the whole substance of his life, yet with all the gain he got thereby, being never wasteful spender thereof, he was not able, after the resignation of his office of Lord Chancellor, for the maintenance of himself and such as necessarily belonged unto him, sufficiently to find meat, drink, fuel, apparel, and such other necessary charges. All the land that ever he purchased—which also he purchased before he was Lord Chancellor—was not, I am well assured, above the value of twenty marks by the year : and after his debts paid, he had not, I know, his chain excepted, in gold and silver left him the worth of one hundred pounds. And whereas upon the holy-

53

days, during his high chancellorship, one of his gentlemen, when service at the church was done, ordinarily used to come to my lady his wife's pew-door, and say unto her, " Madam, my lord is gone," the next holyday after the surrender of his office and departure of his gentlemen, he came unto my lady his wife's pew himself, and making a low courtesy, said unto her, " Madam, my lord is gone." But she, thinking this at first to be but one of his jests, was little moved, till he told her sadly he had given up the great seal. Whereupon she speaking some passionate words, he called his daughters then present to see if they could not spy some fault about their mother's dressing, but they, after search, saying they could find none, he replied, " do you not perceive that your mother's nose standeth somewhat awry ?" Of which jeer the provoked lady was so sensible that she went from him in a rage. In the time somewhat before his trouble he would talk unto his wife and children of the joys of heaven and pains of hell, of the lives of holy martyrs, of their grievous martyrdoms, of their marvellous patience, and of their passions and deaths that they suffered rather than they would offend God, and what a happy and blessed thing it was for the love of God to suffer the loss of goods, imprisonment, loss of lands, and life also. He would farther say unto them, that upon his faith, if he might perceive his wife and children would encourage him to die in a good cause, it should so comfort him that for very joy thereof it would make him merrily run to death. He showed to them before what trouble might after fall unto him : wherewith and the like virtuous talk he had so long before his trouble encouraged them, that when he after fell into trouble indeed, his trouble was to them a great deal the less. *Quia spicula prævisa minus lædunt.* Now upon this resignment of his office, came Sir Thomas Cromwell, then in the king's high favour, to Chelsea to him with a message from the king. Wherein when they had thoroughly communed together, "Master Cromwell," quoth he, "you are now entered into the service of a most noble, wise, and liberal prince ; if you will follow my poor advice, you shall, in your counsel-giving to his grace, ever tell him what he ought to do, but never what he is able to do. So shall you show yourself a true faithful servant, and a right wise and worthy counsellor. For if a lion knew his own strength, hard were it for any man to rule him." Shortly thereupon was there a commission directed to Cranmer, then Archbishop of Canterbury, to determine the matter of the matrimony between the king and Queen Katharine, at

St. Alban's, where, according to the king's mind, it was thoroughly determined. Who pretending because he had no justice at the Pope's hands, from thenceforth sequestered himself from the see of Rome, and so married the Lady Anne Bullen. Which Sir Thomas More understanding, said unto me, "God give grace, son, that these matters within a while be not confirmed with oaths." I, at that time, seeing no likelihood thereof, yet fearing lest for his fore-speaking it would the sooner come to pass, waxed therefore for his so saying much offended with him.

IT fortuned not long before the coming of Queen Anne through the streets of London from the Tower to Westminster to her coronation, that he received a letter from the Bishops of Durham, Bath and Winchester, requesting him both to keep them company from the Tower to the coronation, and also to take twenty pounds, that by the bearer thereof they had sent him, to buy a gown withal ; which he thankfully receiving, and at home still tarrying, at their next meeting said merrily unto them ; " My lords, in the letters which you lately sent me you required two things of me : the one, sith I was so well content to grant you, the other therefore I thought I might be the bolder to deny you. And like as the one, because I took you for no beggars, and myself I knew to be no rich man, I thought I might the rather fulfil, so the other did put me in remembrance of an emperor who ordained a law that whosoever had committed a certain heinous offence

57

(which I now remember not), except it were a virgin, should suffer the pains of death—such a reverence had he to virginity. Now so it happened that the first committer of that offence was indeed a virgin, whereof the emperor hearing was in no small perplexity, as he that by some example would fain have had that law put in execution. Whereupon when his council had sat long, solemnly debating this cause, suddenly rose there up one of his council, a good plain man, amongst them, and said, ' Why make you so much ado, my lords, about so small a matter ? let her first be deflowered, and then after may she be devoured.' And so though your lordships have in the matter of the matrimony hitherto kept yourselves pure virgins, yet take good heed, my lords, that you keep your virginity still. For some there be that by procuring your lordships first at the coronation to be present, and next to preach for the setting forth of it, and finally to write books to all the world in defence thereof are desirous to deflower you, and when they have deflowered you, then will they not fail soon after to devour you. Now, my Lords," quoth he, "it lieth not in my power but that they may devour me, but God being my good Lord, I will so provide that they shall never deflower me."

IN continuance: when the king saw that he could by no manner of benefit win him to his side, then lo, went he about by terror and threats to drive him thereunto. The beginning of which trouble grew by occasion of a certain nun dwelling in Canterbury, for her virtue and holiness of life among the people not a little esteemed : unto whom, for that cause, many religious persons, doctors of divinity, and divers others of good worship of the laity used to resort. Who affirming that she had revelations from God to give the king warning of his wicked life, and of the abuse of the sword and authority committed to him by God, and understanding my Lord of Rochester, Bishop Fisher, to be a man of notable virtuous living and learning, repaired to Rochester, and there disclosed unto him all her revelations, desiring his advice and council therein. Which the bishop perceiving might well stand with the laws of God and His holy church, advised her

59

(as she before had warning and intended) to go to
the king herself, and to let him know and understand the whole circumstance thereof. Whereupon
she went to the king and told him all her revelations,
and so returned home again. And in short space
after, making a journey to the nuns of Sion, by
means of one Master Raynolds, a father of the same
house, she there fortuned, concerning such secrets
as had been revealed unto her (some part whereof
seemed to touch the matter of the king's supremacy
and marriage which shortly followed), to enter into
talk with Sir Thomas More. Who, notwithstanding
he might well at that time without danger of any
law—though after, as himself had prognosticated
before, those matters were established by statutes
and confirmed by oaths—freely and safely have
talked with her therein, nevertheless in all the communication between them (as in process it appeared)
had always so discreetly demeaned himself, that he
deserved not to be blamed, but contrariwise to be
commended and praised. And had he not been one
that in all his great offices and doings for the king
and the realm, so many years together, had from all
corruption and wrong-doing or bribes-taking kept himself so clear, that no man was able therewith once
to blame or blemish him, or make any just quarrel

against him, it would without doubt in this troublous time of the king's indignation towards him have been deeply laid to his charge, and of the king's highness most favourably accepted. As in the case of one Parnell it most manifestly appeared ; against whom, because Sir Thomas More while he was Lord Chancellor, at the suit of one Vaughan his adversary, had made a decree, this Parnell to his highness most grievously complained that he, for making the decree, had of the said Vaughan, unable to travel abroad himself for the gout, by the hands of his wife taken a fair great gilt cup for a bribe. Who thereupon, by the king's appointment being called before the whole council where the matter was heinously laid to his charge, forthwith confessed that forasmuch as that cup was, long after the foresaid decree, brought him for a New Year's gift, he, upon her importunate pressing upon him thereof, of courtesy refused not to receive it. Then the Lord of Wiltshire, for hatred of his religion preferrer of this suit, with much re-joicing said unto the lords : "Lo, my lords, did I not tell you, my lords, that you should find this matter true ?" Whereupon Sir Thomas More de-sired their lordships that as they had heard him courteously tell the one part of his tale, so that they would vouchsafe of their honours indifferently to hear the other. After which obtained, he farther declared unto them, that albeit he had indeed with much work received that cup, yet immediately thereupon caused he his butler to fill it with wine, and of that cup drank to her; and that when he had so done and she pledged him, then as freely as her husband had given it to him even so freely gave he the same again to her to give unto her husband for his New Year's gift: which, at his instant request, though much against her will, at length yet she was fain to receive, as herself and certain others there present before them deposed. Thus was the great mountain turned scant to a little molehill. So I remember that at another time, upon a New Year's day, there came unto him one Mistress Croker, a rich widow, for whom with no small pains he had made a decree in the Chancery against the Lord of Arundel, to present him with a pair of gloves and forty pounds in angels in them for a New Year's gift. Of whom he thankfully receiving the gloves, but refusing the money, said unto her: "Mistress, since it were against good manners to forsake a gentlewoman's New Year's gift, I am content to take your gloves, but as for your money I utterly refuse." So, much against her mind, enforced he her to take her gold again. And one Master Gresham likewise at the same time, having a cause depending in the Chancery before him, sent him for New Year's gift a fair gilt cup, the fashion whereof he very well liking, caused one of his own, though not in his fantasy of so good a fashion yet better in value, to be brought out of his chamber, which he willed the messenger, in recompense to deliver unto his master, and under other conditions would he in no wise receive it. Many things more of like effect, for the declaration of his innocency and clearness from all corruption or evil affection, could I here rehearse besides, which for tediousness omitting, I refer to the readers by these few fore-remembered examples with their own judgments wisely to weigh and consider.

AT the parliament following was there put into the Lords' house a bill to attaint the nun, and divers other religious persons, of high treason, and the Bishop of Rochester, Sir Thomas More, and certain others of misprision of treason ; the king presupposing of likelihood that this bill would be to Sir Thomas More so troublous and terrible that it would force him to relent and condescend to his request ; wherein his grace was much deceived. To which bill Sir Thomas More was a suitor personally to be received in his own defence to make answer. But the king not liking that, assigned the Bishop of Canterbury, the Lord Chancellor, the Duke of Norfolk, and Master Cromwell, at a day and place appointed, to call Sir Thomas More before them. At which time I, thinking that I had a good and fit opportunity, earnestly advised him to labour to those lords for the help of his discharge out of the parliament bill. Who answered me he would. And at his

64

coming before them, according to their appointment, they entertained him very friendly, willing him to sit down with them, which in no wise he would. Then began the Lord Chancellor to declare unto him how many ways the king had showed his love and favour towards him ; how fain he would have had him continue in his office ; how glad he would have been to have heaped more benefits upon him ; and finally how he could ask no worldly honour nor profit at his highness' hands that were likely to be denied him ; hoping, by the declaration of the king's kindness and affection towards him, to provoke him to recompense his grace with the like again, and unto those things which the parliament, the bishops, and the Universities had already passed, to add his consent. To this Sir Thomas More mildly made answer, saying, " No man living is there, my lords, that would with better will do the thing that should be acceptable to the king's highness than I, which must needs confess his manifold benefits and bountiful goodness, most benignly bestowed upon me. Howbeit, I verily hoped I should never have heard of this matter more, considering that I have from time to time always from the beginning, so plainly and truly declared my mind unto his grace, which his highness ever seemed to me, like a most gracious prince, very well to accept, never minding, as he said, to molest me more therewith. Since which time any further thing that was able to move me to any change could I never find ; and if I could, there is none in all the world that would have been gladder of it than I." Many things more were there of like sort uttered on both sides. But in the end, when they saw they could by no manner of persuasions remove him from his former determination, then began they more terribly to touch him, telling him that the king's highness had given them in commandment if they could by no gentleness win him, in his name with his great ingratitude to charge him, that never was there servant to his sovereign so villainous, nor subject to his prince so traitorous as he. For he by his subtle sinister sleights most unnaturally procuring and provoking him to set forth a book of the assertion of the seven sacraments and maintenance of the Pope's authority, had caused him, to his dishonour throughout all Christendom, to put a sword in the Pope's hand to fight against himself. When they had thus laid forth all the terrors they could imagine against him : " My lords," quoth he, " these terrors be arguments for children, and not for me. But to answer that wherewith you do chiefly burthen me, I believe the king's highness of his honour will never lay that to my charge, or none is there that can in that point say in my excuse more than his highness himself, who right well knoweth that I was never procurer nor counsellor of his majesty thereunto, but after it was finished, by his grace's appointment and consent of the makers of the same, I was only a sorter out and placer of the principal matters therein contained. Wherein when I found the pope's authority highly advanced, and with strong arguments mightily defended, I said unto his grace, 'I must put your highness in remembrance of one thing, and that is this; the Pope, as your grace knoweth, is a prince as you are, and in league with all other Christian princes: it may here after so fall out that your grace and he may vary upon some points of the league, whereupon may grow breach of amity and war between you both; I think it best therefore that that place be amended, and his authority more slenderly touched.' 'Nay,' quoth his grace, 'that it shall not: we are so much bounden unto the see of Rome that we cannot do too much honour unto it.' Then did I farther put him in remembrance of the Statute of Præmunire, whereby a good part of the Pope's pastoral care here was pared away. To that answered his highness: 'Whatsoever impediment be to the contrary, we will set forth that authority to

67

the uttermost, for we received from that see our crown imperial'; which I never heard of before till his grace told it me with his own mouth. So that I trust when his grace shall be truly informed of this, and call to his gracious remembrance my doing in that behalf, his highness will never speak of it more, but clear me therein thoroughly himself." And thus displeasantly departed they. Then took Sir Thomas More his boat towards his house at Chelsea, wherein by the way he was very merry, and for that I was nothing sorry, hoping that he had gotten himself discharged out of the parliament bill. When he was landed and come home, then walked we twain alone in his garden together : where I, desirous to know how he had sped, said : " I trust, Sir, that all is well because that you be so merry." " It is so indeed, son Roper, I thank God," quoth he. " Are you then put out of the parliament bill ?" quoth I. " By my troth, son Roper," quoth he, " I never rememembered it !" " Never remembered it !" said I, " a case that toucheth yourself so near, and us all for your sake ! I am sorry to hear it, for I verily trusted, when I saw you so merry, that all had been well." Then said he : " Wilt thou know, son Roper, why I was so merry ?" " That would I gladly, Sir," quoth I. " In good faith I rejoiced, son," said he, " that I had

68

given the devil a foul fall, and that with those lords I had gone so far as without great shame I could never go back again." At which words waxed I very sad ; for though himself liked it well, yet liked it me but a little. Now upon the report made by the Lord Chancellor and the other lords to the king of all their whole discourse had with Sir Thomas More, the king was so highly offended with him, he plainly told them he was fully determined that the foresaid parliament bill should undoubtedly proceed forth against him. To whom the Lord Chancellor and the rest of the lords said, that they perceived the lords of the upper house so precisely bent to hear him, in his own defence, make answer himself, that if he were not put out of the bill, it would, without fail, be utterly an overthrow of all. But for all this, needs would the king have his own will therein, or else, he said that at the passing thereof he would be personally present himself. Then the Lord Audley and the rest, seeing him so vehemently set thereupon, on their knees, most humbly besought his grace to forbear the same, considering that if he should in his own presence receive an overthrow, it would not only encourage his subjects ever after to contemn him, but also through all Christendom redound to his dishonour for ever : adding thereunto that they mistrusted not in time against him to find some meeter matter to serve his grace's turn better; for in this cause of the nun he was accounted, they said, so innocent and clear, that for his dealing therein, men reckoned him far worthier of praise than reproof.. Whereupon, at length, through their earnest persuasion, he was content to condescend to their petition; and on the morrow, after Master Cromwell meeting me in the parliament house, willed me to tell my father that he was put out of the parliament bill. But because I had appointed to dine that day in London, I sent the message by my servant to my wife to Chelsea. Whereof when she informed her father: "In faith, Megg," quoth he, "*Quod differtur non aufertur.*" After this, as the Duke of Norfolk and Sir Thomas More chanced to fall in familiar talk together, the Duke said unto him: "By the mass, Master More, it is perilous striving with princes, therefore I would wish you somewhat to incline to the king's pleasure. For by God's body, Master More, *Indignatio principis mors est.*" ' "Is that all, my lord?" quoth he. ' "Then in good faith the difference between your grace and me is but this, that *I shall die to-day and you to-morrow*" So fell it out, within a month or thereabout, after the making of the Statute for the Oath of the Supremacy and

70

Matrimony, that all the priests of London and West-minster, and no temporal men but he, were sent for to appear at Lambeth before the Bishop of Canterbury, the Lord Chancellor, and Secretary Cromwell, commissioners appointed there to tender the oath unto them. Then Sir Thomas More, as his accustomed manner was always ere he entered into any matter of importance—as when he was first chosen of the king's privy council, when he was sent ambassador, appointed Speaker of the Parliament, made Lord Chancellor, or when he took any like weighty matter upon him—to go to church and be confessed, to hear mass, and be houseled, so did he likewise in the morning early the selfsame day that he was summoned to appear before the lords at Lambeth. And whereas he evermore used before, at his departure from his wife and children, whom he tenderly loved, to have them bring him to his boat, and there to kiss them, and bid them all farewell, then would he suffer none of them forth of the gate to follow him, but pulled the wicket after him, and shut them all from him, and with a heavy heart, as by his countenance it appeared, with me and our four servants there took boat towards Lambeth. Wherein sitting still sadly a while, at the last he rounded me in the ear and said: " Son Roper, I thank our Lord

71

the field is won." What he meant thereby I wist not, yet loath to seem ignorant, I answered : " Sir, I am thereof very glad." But, as I conjectured afterwards, it was for that the love he had to God wrought in him so effectually, that it conquered all his carnal affections utterly. Now at his coming to Lambeth, how wisely he behaved himself before the commissioners at the ministration of the oath unto him may be found in certain Letters of his sent to my wife remaining in a great book of his works. Where by the space of four days he was betaken to the custody of the Abbot of Westminster, during which time the king consulted with his council what order were meet to be taken with him. And albeit in the beginning they were resolved that with an oath, not to be acknown, whether he had to the supremacy been sworn, or what he thought thereof, he should be discharged ; yet did Queen Anne by her importunate clamour so sore exasperate the king against him, that, contrary to his former resolution, he caused the said Oath of the Supremacy to be ministered unto him. Who albeit he made a discreet qualified answer, nevertheless was committed to the Tower. Who as he was going thitherward wearing, as he commonly did, a chain of gold about his neck, Sir Richard Cromwell, that had the charge of his conveyance thither, advised him to send home his chain to his wife or to some of his children. "Nay, Sir," quoth he, "that I will not : for if I were taken in the field by my enemies I would they should somewhat fare the better for me." At whose landing Master Lieutenant was ready at the Tower gate to receive him, where the porter demanded of him his upper garment. "Master porter," quoth he, "here it is," and took off his cap and delivered it to him, saying, "I am very sorry it is no better for thee." "No, Sir," quoth the porter, "I must have your gown." And so was he by Master Lieutenant conveyed to his lodging, where he called unto him one John a Wood, his own servant there appointed to attend him, who could neither write nor read, and sware him before the lieutenant, that if he should hear or see him at any time speak or write any matter against the king, the council, or the state or the realm, he should open it to the lieutenant, that the lieutenant might incontinent reveal it to the council.

NOW when he had remained in the Tower little more than a month, my wife, longing to see her father, by her earnest suit at length got leave to go unto him. At whose coming after the seven psalms and litany said—which whensoever she came to him, ere he fell in talk of any worldly matters, he used accustomedly to say with her—among other communication he said unto her: " I believe, Megg, that they that have put me here ween that they have done me a high displeasure : but I assure thee on my faith, mine own good daughter, if it had not been for my wife and ye that be my children (whom I account the chief part of my charge) I would not have failed long ere this to have closed myself in as straight a room, and straighter too. But since I am come hither without mine own desert, I trust that God of His goodness will discharge me of my care, and with His gracious help supply my lack among you. I find no cause, I thank God, Megg, to reckon myself

74

in worse case here than in mine own house, for me thinketh God maketh me a wanton, and setteth me on his lap and dandleth me." Thus, by his gracious demeanour in tribulation, appeared it that all the trouble that ever chanced unto him, by his patient sufferance thereof, were to him no painful punishments, but of his patience profitable exercises. And at another time, when he had first questioned with my wife a while of the order of his wife, children, and state of his house in his absence, he asked her how Queen Anne did. "In faith, Father," quoth she, "never better." "Never better, Megg!" quoth he, "alas! Megg, alas! it pitieth me to remember into what misery, poor soul, she shall shortly come." After this Master Lieutenant coming into his chamber to visit him, rehearsed the benefits and friendship that he had many ways received at his hands, and how much bounden he was therefore friendly to entertain him, and to make him good cheer ; which since, the case standing as it did, he could do not without the king's indignation, he trusted he said, he would accept his good will, and such poor cheer as he had. "Master Lieutenant," quoth he again, "I verily believe as you say, so are you my good friend indeed, and would, as you say, with your best cheer entertain me, for the which I

75

most heartily thank you : and assure yourself, Master Lieutenant, I do not mislike my cheer, but whensoever I so do, then thrust me out of your doors." Whereas the oath confirming the Supremacy and Matrimony was by the first statute in few words comprised, the Lord Chancellor and Mr. Secretary did of their own heads add more words unto it, to make it appear to the king's ears more pleasant and plausible, and that oath, so amplified, caused they to be ministered to Sir Thomas More, and to all other throughout the realm. Which Sir Thomas More perceiving, said unto my wife : " I may tell thee, Megg, they that have committed me hither for the refusing of this oath, not agreeable with the statute, are not by their own law able to justify mine imprisonment : and surely, daughter, it is great pity that any Christian prince should by a flexible council ready to follow his affections, and by a weak clergy lacking grace constantly to stand to their learning, with flattery be so shamefully abused." But, at length, the Lord Chancellor and Mr. Secretary, espying their oversight in that behalf, were fain afterward to find the means that another statute should be made for the confirmation of the oath so amplified with their additions.

AFTER Sir Thomas More had given over his office, and all worldly doings therewith, to the intent he might from thenceforth settle himself the more quietly to the service of God, then made he a conveyance for the disposition of all his lands, reserving to himself an estate thereof only for term of his own life : and after his decease assuring some part thereof to his wife, some to his son's wife for a jointure in consideration that she was an inheretrix in possession of more than a hundred pounds land by the year, and some to me and my wife in recompense of our marriage money, with divers remainders over. All which conveyance and assurance was perfectly finished long before the matter whereupon he was attainted was made an offence, and yet after by statute clearly avoided ; and so were all his lands that he had to his wife and children by the said conveyance in such sort assured, contrary to the order of law, taken from them and brought into the king's hands, saving that portion

77

which he had appointed to my wife and me. Which
although he had in the foresaid conveyance reserved
as he did the rest for term of life to himself, nevertheless upon consideration two days after by another
conveyance he gave the same immediately to my wife
and me in possession : and so because the statute had
undone only the first conveyance, giving no more to
the king but so much as passed by that, the second
conveyance, whereby it was given to my wife and me,
being dated two days after, was without the compass
of the statute, and so was our portion by that means
clearly reserved to us. As Sir Thomas More, in the
Tower, chanced on a time, looking out of his win-
dow, to behold one Master Reynolds, a religious,
learned and virtuous father of Sion, and three monks
of the Charterhouse, for the matter of the Supremacy
and Matrimony, going out of the Tower to execution,
he, as one longing in that journey to have accom-
panied them, said unto my wife, then standing there
beside him : " Lo, doest thou not see, Megg, that
these blessed fathers be now as cheerfully going to
their deaths as bridegrooms to their marriage ?
Wherefore thereby mayest thou see, mine own good
daughter, what a great difference there is between
such as have in effect spent all their days in a straight,
hard, penitential and painful life, religiously, and

such as have in the world, like worldly wretches, as thy poor father hath done, consumed all their time in pleasure and ease licentiously. For God, considering their long continued life in most sore and grievous penance, will no longer suffer them to remain here in this vale of misery and iniquity, but speedily hence taketh them to the fruition of His everlasting Deity. Whereas thy silly father, Megg, that like a most wicked caitiff hath passed forth the whole course of his miserable life most sinfully, God, thinking him not worthy so soon to come to that eternal felicity, leaveth him here yet still in the world further to be plagued and turmoiled with misery." Within a while after Master Secretary coming to him into the Tower from the King, pretended much friendship towards him, and for his comfort told him, that the king's highness was his good and gracious lord, and mindeth not with any matter wherein he should have any cause of scruple henceforth to trouble his conscience. As soon as Master Secretary was gone, to express what comfort he received of his words, he wrote with a coal, for ink then he had none, these verses :

Eye-flatt'ring fortune, look thou ne'er so fair,
Or ne'er so pleasantly begin to smile,
As though thou wouldst my ruin all repair,

79

)uring my life thou shall not me beguile
ſrust shall I, God, to enter in a while,
ſhy haven of heaven sure and uniform,
ɔ'er after thy calm look I for a storm.

WHEN Sir Thomas More had continued a good while in the Tower, my lady, his wife, obtained license to see him. Who, at her first coming, like a simple ignorant woman, and somewhat worldly too, with this manner of salutation bluntly saluted him : "What the good-yere, Master More," quoth she, "I marvel that you that have been always hitherto taken for so wise a man will now so play the fool to lie here in this close filthy prison, and be content thus to be shut up among mice and rats, when you might be abroad at your liberty, and with the favour and good will both of the king and his council if you would but do as all the bishops and best learned of this realm have done. And seeing you have at Chelsea a right fair house, your library, your gallery, your garden, your orchard, and all other necessaries so handsome about you, where you might in the company of me your wife, your children, and household, be merry, I muse what a God's name you mean here still thus fondly to tarry." After he had a while quietly heard her, with a cheerful countenance he said unto her: "I pray thee, good Mistress Alice, tell me one thing!" "What is that?" quoth she. "Is not this house," quoth he, "as nigh heaven as mine own?" To whom she after her accustomed homely fashion, not liking such talk, answered: "Tylle valle, Tylle valle!" "How say you, Mistress Alice, is it not so?" "*Bone Deus, bone Deus,* man, will this gear never be left?" quoth she. "Well then, Mistress Alice, if it be so," quoth he, "it is very well. For I see no great cause why I should much joy in my gay house, or in any thing thereunto belonging, when if I should but seven years lie buried under the ground and then arise and come thither again, I should not fail to find some therein that would bid me get out of doors, and tell me it were none of mine. What cause have I then to like such a house as would so soon forget his master?" So her persuasions moved him but a little. Not long after came to him the Lord Chancellor, the Dukes of Norfolk and Suffolk, with Master Secretary, and certain other of the privy council, at two several times by all policies possible procuring him either precisely to confess the Supremacy, or precisely to deny it, whereunto, as appeareth by his examinations in the said great book, they could never bring him. Shortly thereupon Master Rich, afterward Lord Rich, then newly made the King's Solicitor, Sir Richard Southwell, and one Master Palmer, servant to the Secretary, were sent to Sir Thomas More into the Tower to fetch away his books from him. And while Sir Richard Southwell and Mr. Palmer were busy in the trussing up of his books, Mr. Rich, pretending friendly talk with him, among other things of a set course, as it seemed, said thus unto him : "Forasmuch as it is well known, Master More, that you are a man both wise and well learned as well in the laws of the realm as otherwise, I pray you therefore, Sir, let me be so bold, as of good will, to put unto you this case. Admit there were, Sir," quoth he, "an act of parliament that the realm should take me for king, would not you, Mr. More, take me for king ?" "Yes, Sir," quoth Sir Thomas More, "that would I." "I put the case further," quoth Mr. Rich, "that there were an act of parliament that all the realm should take me for pope, would you not then, Master More, take me for pope ?" "For answer, Sir," quoth Sir Thomas More, "to your first case, the parliament may well, Master Rich, meddle with the state of temporal princes, but to make answer to your other case, I will put you this case : suppose the parliament would make a law that God should not be God, would you then, Master Rich, say that God were not God ?" "No, Sir," quoth he, "that would I not, sith no parliament may make any such law." "No more," said Sir Thomas More (as Master Rich reported him), "could the parliament make the king supreme head of the church." Upon whose only report was Sir Thomas More indicted of high treason on the Statute to deny the king to be Supreme Head of the Church, into which indictment were put these heinous words, *maliciously*, *traitorously* and *diabolically*.

WHEN Sir Thomas More was brought from the Tower to Westminster Hall to answer to the indictment, and at the King's Bench bar there before the judges arraigned, he openly told them that he would upon that indictment have abiden in law, but that he thereby should have been driven to confess of himself the matter indeed, that was the denial of the king's supremacy, which he protested was untrue. Wherefore he thereunto pleaded not guilty, and so reserved unto himself advantage to be taken of the body of the matter after verdict to avoid that indictment : and moreover added, that if those only odious terms, *maliciously*, *traitorously*, and *diabolically*, were put out of the indictment, he saw therein nothing justly to charge him. And for proof to the jury that Sir Thomas More was guilty of this treason Master Rich was called forth to give evidence unto them upon his oath, as he did : against whom thus sworn, Sir Thomas More began in this wise to say :

" If I were a man, my lords, that did not regard an oath I needed not, as it is well known, in this place, and at this time, nor in this case to stand here as an accused person. And if this oath of yours, Master Rich, be true, then I pray that I never see God in the face, which I would not say, were it otherwise, to win the whole world." Then recited he to the court the discourse of all their communication in the Tower according to the truth, and said : " In good faith, Master Rich, I am sorrier for your perjury than for mine own peril, and you shall understand that neither I nor no man else to my knowledge, ever took you to be a man of such credit as in any matter of importance I or any other would at any time vouchsafe to communicate with you. And I, as you know, of no small while have been acquainted with you and your conversation, who have known you from your youth hitherto, for we long dwelled together in one parish. Whereas yourself can tell—I am sorry you compel me to say—you were esteemed very light of your tongue, a great dicer, and of no commendable fame. And so in your house at the Temple, where hath been your chief bringing up, were you likewise accounted. Can it therefore seem likely unto your honourable lordships that I would in so weighty a cause so unadvisedly overshoot myself as to trust

Master Rich, a man of me always reputed of so little truth, as your lordships have heard, so far above my sovereign lord the king, or any of his noble counsellors, that I would unto him utter the secrets of my conscience touching the king's Supremacy, the special point and only mark at my hands so long sought for? A thing which I never did, nor never would, after the statute thereof made, reveal unto the king's highness himself or to any of his honourable counsellors, as it is not unknown unto your honours at sundry and several times sent from his grace's own person to the Tower unto me for none other purpose. Can this in your judgment, my lords, seem likely to be true? And if I had so done indeed, my lords, as Master Rich hath sworn, seeing it was spoken but in familiar secret talk, nothing affirming, and only in putting of cases, without other displeasant circumstances, it cannot justly be taken to be spoken *maliciously* : and where there is no malice, there can be no offence. And over this I can never think, my lords, that so many worthy bishops, so many honourable personages, and many other worshipful, virtuous, wise and well learned men, as at the making of that law were in the parliament assembled, ever meant to have any man punished by death in whom there could be found no malice, taking *malitia* for *malevolentia* : for if

87

malitia be generally taken for sin, no man is there then that can excuse himself. *Quia si dixerimus quod peccatum non habemus, nosmet ipsos seducemus, et veritas in nobis non est.* And only this word *maliciously* is in the statute material, as this term *forcibly* is in the statute of *forcible entries*, by which statute if a man enter peaceably, and put not his adversary out *forcibly*, it is no offence, but if he put him out *forcibly*, then by that statute it is an offence, and so shall he be punished by this term *forcibly*. Besides this, the manifold goodness of the king's highness himself, that hath been so many ways my singular good lord and gracious sovereign, and that hath so dearly loved and trusted me, even at my very first coming into his noble service, with the dignity of his honourable Privy Council vouchsafing to admit me, and to offices of great credit and worship most liberally advanced me ; and finally with that weighty room of his grace's high chancellor, the like whereof he never did to temporal man before, next to his own royal person the highest officer in this whole realm, so far above my qualities or merits able and meet therefore of his own incomparable benignity honoured and exalted me ; by the space of twenty years and more, showing his continual favour toward me, and (until at mine own poor suit it pleased his highness giving me license with his majesty's favour to bestow the residue of my life, for the provision of my soul, in the service of God, and of his special goodness thereof to discharge and unburthen me) most benignly heaped honours continually more and more upon me : all this his highness' goodness, I say, so long thus bountifully extended towards me, were in my mind, my lords, matter sufficient to convince this slanderous surmise by this man so wrongfully imagined against me." Master Rich, seeing himself so disproved, and his credit so foully defaced, caused Sir Richard Southwell and Master Palmer, who at the time of their communication were in the chamber, to be sworn what words had passed betwixt them. Whereupon Master Palmer upon his depositions said, that " he was so busy about trussing up Sir Thomas More's books into a sack that he took no heed to their talk." Sir Richard Southwell likewise said upon his deposition, that " because he was appointed only to look to the conveyance of those books he gave no ear to them." After this were there many other reasons, not now in my remembrance, by Sir Thomas More in his own defence alleged to the discredit of Master Rich's foresaid evidence, and proof of the clearness of his own conscience ; all which notwithstanding, the jury found him guilty. And incontinent upon their verdict the Lord Chancellor, for that matter Chief Commissioner, beginning to proceed in judgment against him, Sir Thomas More said unto him : " My Lord, when I was toward the law, the manner in such case was to ask the prisoner before judgment what he could say, why judgment should not be given against him."   Whereupon the Lord Chancellor, staying his judgment, wherein he had partly proceeded, demanded of him what he was able to say to the contrary.   Who then in this sort most humbly made answer :

"FORASMUCH, my Lord," quoth he, " as this indictment is grounded upon an act of parliament directly repugnant to the laws of God and His holy Church, the supreme government of which, or any part thereof, may no temporal prince presume by any law to take upon him, as rightfully belonging to the see of Rome, a spiritual pre-eminence by the mouth of our Saviour himself, personally present upon the earth, only to Saint Peter and his successors, bishops of the same see, by special prerogative granted ; it is therefore in law, amongst Christian men, insufficient to charge any Christian man." And for proof thereof, like as amongst divers other reasons and authorities, he declared that this realm, being but a member and small part of the church, might not make a particular law disagreeable with the general law of Christ's universal Catholic Church, no more than the City of London, being but one poor member in respect of the whole realm, might make a law against an act of parliament to bind the whole realm : so further showed he that it was both contrary to the laws and statutes of this our land yet unrepealed, as they might evidently perceive in MAGNA CHARTA, *quod* Ecclesia Anglicana *libera sit, et habeat omnia jura sua integra, et libertates suas illæsas,* and also contrary to that sacred oath which the king's highness himself, and every other Christian prince, always with great solemnity received at their coronations.   Alleging, moreover, that no more might this realm of England refuse obedience to the See of Rome, than might the child refuse obedience to his natural father.   For, as St. Paul said to the Corinthians, *I have regenerated you, my children in Christ,* so might St. Gregory, Pope of Rome (of whom, by St. Augustine his messenger, we first received the Christian faith) of us Englishmen truly say, You are my children, because I have under Christ given to you everlasting salvation (a far higher and better inheritance than any carnal father can leave to his child), and by regeneration have made you spiritual children in Christ.   Then was it by the Lord Chancellor thereunto answered, that, " seeing all the bishops, universities, and best learned men of the realm had to this act agreed, it was much marvelled that he alone against them all would so stiffly stick thereat, and so vehemently argue there-against." To that Sir Thomas More replied, saying: "If the number of bishops and universities be so material as your lordship seemeth to take it, then see I little cause, my lord, why that thing in my conscience should make any change. For I nothing doubt but that, though not in this realm, yet in Christendom about, of these well learned bishops and virtuous men that are yet alive, they be not the fewer part that be of my mind therein. But if I should speak of those that already be dead, of whom many be now holy saints in heaven, I am very sure it is the far, far greater part of them that all the while they lived thought in this case that way that I now think; and therefore am I not bound, my lord, to conform my conscience to the council of one realm, against the general council of Christendom."

NOW when Sir Thomas More for the avoiding of the indictment had taken as many exceptions as he thought meet, and many more reasons than I can now remember alleged, the Lord Chancellor, loth to have the burden of the judgment wholly to depend upon himself, there openly asked the advice of the Lord Fitzjames, then Lord Chief Justice of the King's Bench, and joined in commission with him, whether this indictment were sufficient or not. Who, like a wise man answered, "My Lords all, by St. Julian" (that was ever his oath) "I must needs confess that if the act of parliament be not unlawful, then is the indictment in my conscience not insufficient." Whereupon the Lord Chancellor said to the rest of the Lords : "Lo, my Lords, lo ! you hear what my Lord Chief Justice saith," and so immediately gave judgment against him. After which ended, the commissioners yet further courteously offered him, if he had anything else to allege for his defence, to grant him favourable audience. Who answered : " More have I not to say, my Lords, but that like as the blessed apostle St. Paul, as we read in the Acts of the Apostles, was present and consented to the death of St. Stephen, and kept their clothes that stoned him to death, and yet be they now both twain holy saints in heaven, and shall continue there friends for ever, so I verily trust, and shall therefore right heartily pray, that though your lordships have now here in earth been judges to my condemnation, we may yet hereafter in heaven merrily all meet together to everlasting salvation." Thus much touching Sir Thomas More's arraignment, being not there present myself, have I by the credible report of the Right Worshipful Sir Anthony Saint-leger, and partly of Richard Haywood, and John Webb, gentlemen, with others of good credit at the hearing thereof present themselves, as far forth as my poor wit and memory would serve me, here truly rehearsed unto you. Now, after his arraignment, departed he from the bar to the Tower again, led by Sir William Kingston, a tall, strong, and comely knight, Constable of the Tower, and his very dear friend. Who when he had brought him from West-minster to the Old Swan towards the Tower, there with a heavy heart, the tears running down his cheeks, bade him farewell. Sir Thomas More, seeing him so sorrowful, comforted him with as good words as he could, saying : "Good Master Kingston, trouble not yourself, but be of good cheer : for 1 will pray for you and my good lady your wife, that we may meet in heaven together, where we shall be merry for ever and ever." Soon after Sir William Kingston, talking with me of Sir Thomas More, said : "In good faith, Mr. Roper, I was ashamed of myself that at my departing from your father I found my heart so feeble and his so strong, that he was fain to comfort me that should rather have comforted him." When Sir Thomas More came from Westminster to the Tower-ward again, his daughter, my wife, desirous to see her father, whom she thought she would never see in this world after, and also to have his final blessing, gave attendance about the Tower Wharf, where she knew he should pass by, before he could enter into the Tower. There tarrying his coming, as soon as she saw him, after his blessing upon her knees reverently received, she hasting towards him, without consideration or care of herself, pressing in amongst the midst of the throng and company of the guard, that with halberds and bills went round about him, hastily ran to him, and there openly in sight of them all, embraced him, and took him about the neck and kissed him. Who well liking her most natural and dear daughterly affection towards him, gave her his fatherly blessing, and many godly words of comfort besides. From whom after she was departed, she not satisfied with the former sight of her dear father, and like one that had forgotten herself, being all ravished with the entire love of her dear father, having respect neither to herself, nor to the press of people and multitude that were there about him, suddenly turned back again, ran to him as before, took him about the neck, and divers times kissed him most lovingly ; and at last, with a full and heavy heart, was fain to depart from him : the beholding whereof was to many of them that were present thereat so lamentable, that it made them for very sorrow thereof to weep and mourn.

SO remained Sir Thomas More in the Tower, more than a seven-night after his judgment. From whence, the day before he suffered, he sent his shirt of hair, not willing to have it seen, to my wife, his dearly beloved daughter, and a letter written with a coal (contained in the foresaid book of his works), plainly expressing the fervent desire he had to suffer on the morrow, in these words following : "I cumber you, good Margret, much, but would be sorry if it should be any longer than to-morrow. For to-morrow is St. Thomas even, and the Utas of St. Peter, and therefore to-morrow I long to go to God : it were a day very meet and convenient for me. Dear Megg, I never liked your manner better towards me than when you kissed me last. For I like when daughterly love and dear charity hath no leisure to look to worldly courtesy." And so upon the next morrow, being Tuesday, Saint Thomas his eve, and the Utas of Saint Peter, in the year of our Lord

1535, according as he in his letter the day before had wished, early in the morning came to him Sir Thomas Pope, his singular good friend, on message from the king and his council, that he should before nine of the clock of the same morning suffer death; and that, therefore, he should forthwith prepare himself thereto. "Master Pope," quoth Sir Thomas More, "for your good tidings I heartily thank you. I have been always much bounden to the king's highness for the benefits and honours that he had still from time to time most bountifully heaped upon me; and yet more bounden am I to his grace for putting me into this place, where I have had convenient time and space to have remembrance of my end. And so help me God, most of all, Master Pope, am I bounden to his highness that it pleaseth him so shortly to rid me out of the miseries of this wretched world, and therefore will I not fail earnestly to pray for his grace, both here, and also in the world to come." "The king's pleasure is farther," quoth Master Pope, "that at your execution you shall not use many words." "Master Pope," quoth he, "you do well to give me warning of his grace's pleasure, for otherwise, at that time, had I purposed somewhat to have spoken; but of no matter wherewith his grace, or any other, should have had cause to be

99

offended. Nevertheless, whatsoever I intended, I am ready obediently to conform myself to his grace's commandment ; and I beseech you, good Master Pope, to be a mean to his highness, that my daughter Margaret may be at my burial." "The king is content already," quoth Master Pope, "that your wife, children and other friends shall have liberty to be present thereat." "Oh, how much beholden then," said Sir Thomas More, "am I unto his grace, that unto my poor burial vouchsafeth to have so gracious consideration !" Wherewithal Master Pope, taking his leave of him, could not refrain from weeping. Which Sir Thomas More perceiving, comforted him in this wise : "Quiet yourself, good Master Pope, and be not discomforted, for I trust that we shall once in heaven see each other full merrily, where we shall be sure to live and love together, in joyful bliss eternally." Upon whose departure, Sir Thomas More, as one that had been invited to some solemn feast, changed himself into his best apparel. Which Master Lieutenant espying, advised him to put it off, saying, that he that should have it was but a javill. "What, Master Lieutenant?" quoth he, "shall I account him a javill that will do me this day so singular a benefit ? Nay, I assure you, were it cloth of gold, I should think it well bestowed on him, as Saint Cyprian did, who gave his executioner thirty pieces of gold." And albeit, at length, through Master Lieutenant's importunate persuasion, he altered his apparel, yet, after the example of the holy Martyr St. Cyprian, did he, of that little money that was left him send an angel of gold to his executioner. And so was he by Master Lieutenant brought out of the Tower, and from thence led towards the place of execution. Where, going up the scaffold, which was so weak that it was ready to fall, he said merrily to the Lieutenant : " I pray you, Master Lieutenant, see me safe up, and for my coming down let me shift for myself." Then desired he all the people thereabout to pray for him, and to bear witness with him, that he should now there suffer death in and for the faith of the holy Catholic Church. Which done, he kneeled down, and, after his prayers said, turned to the executioner with a cheerful countenance, and said unto him : " Pluck up thy spirits, man, and be not afraid to do thine office : my neck is very short, take heed, therefore, thou strike not awry, for saving of thine honesty." So passed Sir Thomas More out of this world to God, upon the very same day which he most desired. Soon after his death came intelligence thereof to the Emperor Charles. Whereupon he sent for Sir

Thomas Eliott, our English ambassador, and said to him : "My Lord ambassador, we understand that the king your master hath put his faithful servant, and grave wise councillor, Sir Thomas More, to death." Whereupon Sir Thomas Eliott answered that "he understood nothing thereof." "Well," said the Emperor, "it is too true : and this will we say, that had we been master of such a servant, of whose doings ourselves have had these many years no small experience, we would rather have lost the best city of our dominions, than have lost such a worthy councillor." Which matter was, by the same Sir Thomas Eliott to myself, to my wife, to Master Clement and his wife, to Master John Heywood and his wife, and unto divers others his friends accordingly reported.

THE LETTERS OF
SIR THOMAS MORE
TO HIS DAUGHTER

.

LETTER I

Sir THOMAS MORE'S *Letter to his Daughter Mrs.*
MARGARET ROPER *on his first being made Prisoner in
the Tower of* LONDON, *on Friday the* 17*th day of
April,* 1534. xxv. *Hen.* 8*th.*

WHEN I was before the Lords at Lambeth, I was the
first that was called in, albeit that Master Doctor,
the vicar of Croydon, was come before me, and divers
others. After the cause of my sending for, declared
unto me, (whereof I somewhat marvelled in my mind,
considering that they sent for no more temporal men
but me) I desired the sight of the oath, which they
showed me under the great seal. Then desired I
the sight of the act of the succession, which was
delivered me in a printed roll. After which read
secretly by myself, and the oath considered with the
act, I showed unto them, that my purpose was not
to put any fault, either in the act or any man that
made it, or in the oath or any man that sware it, nor
to condemn the conscience of any other man. But

as for myself in good faith my conscience so moved me in the matter, that though I would not deny to swear to the succession, yet unto that oath that there was offered me, I could not swear without the jeoparding of my soul to perpetual damnation. And that if they doubted whether I did refuse the oath only for the grudge of my conscience, or for any other fantasy, I was ready therein to satisfy them by mine oath. Which if they trusted not, what should they be the better to give me any oath. And if they trusted that I would therein swear true, then trusted I that of their goodness they would not move me to swear the oath that they offered me, perceiving that for to swear it was against my conscience. Unto this my Lord Chancellor said, that they all were very sorry to hear me say thus, and see me thus refuse the oath. And they said all, that on their faith I was the very first that ever refused it ; which would cause the king's highness to conceive great suspicion of me, and great indignation toward me. And therewith they showed me the roll, and let me see the names of the Lords and the Commons which had sworn and subscribed their names already. Which notwithstanding when they saw that I refused to swear the same myself, not blaming any other man that had sworn, I was in conclusion commanded to go down into the garden. And thereupon I tarried in the old burned chamber that looketh into the garden, and would not go down because of the heat. In that time saw I Master Doctor Latimer come into the garden, and there walked he with divers other doctors and chaplains of my Lord of Canterbury. And very merry I saw him, for he laughed, and took one or twain about the neck so handsomely, that if they had been women, I would have weened he had been waxen wanton. After that came Master Doctor Wilson forth from the Lords, and was with two gentlemen brought by me, and gentlemanly sent straight unto the Tower. What time my Lord of Rochester was called in before them, that can I not tell. But at night I heard that he had been before them, but where he remained that night, and so forth, till he was sent hither, I never heard. I heard also that Master Vicar of Croydon, and all the remnant of the priests of London that were sent for, were sworn ; and that they had such favour at the Council's hand, that they were not lingered, nor made to dance any long attendance to their travail and cost, as suitors were sometime wont to be, but were sped apace to their great comfort ; so far forth that Master Vicar of Croydon, either for gladness or for dryness, or else that it might be seen, *Quod ille notus*

erat pontifici, went to my Lord's buttery bar, and
called for drink, and drank *valde familiariter*. When
they had played their pageant, and were gone out of
the place, then was I called in again. And then was
it declared unto me what a number had sworn, ever
since I went aside, gladly without any sticking.
Wherein I laid no blame in no man, but for my
own self answered as before. Now as well before as
then, they somewhat laid unto me for obstinacy, that
whereas before, since I refused to swear, I would not
declare any special part of that oath that grudged
my conscience, and open the cause wherefore. For
thereunto I had said unto them, that I feared lest
the king's highness would, as they said, take displeasure enough toward me, for the only refusal of
the oath. And that if I should open and disclose
the causes why, I should therewith but further exasperate his highness, which I would in no wise do,
but rather would I abide all the danger and harm
that might come toward me, than give his highness
any occasion of further displeasure, than the offering
of the oath unto me of pure necessity constrained
me. Howbeit when they divers times imputed this
to me for stubbornness and obstinacy, that I would
neither swear the oath, nor yet declare the causes
why I declined thus far toward them, that rather

than I would be accounted for obstinate, I would upon the king's gracious licence, or rather his such commandment had, as might be my sufficient warrant, that my declaration should not offend his highness, nor put me in the danger of any of his statutes, I would be content to declare the causes in writing, and over that to give an oath in the beginning that if I might find those causes by any man in such wise answered, as I might think mine own conscience satisfied, I would after that with all mine heart swear the principal oath to. To this I was answered, that though the king would give me licence under his letters patent, yet would it not serve against the statute. Whereto I said, that yet if I had them, I would stand unto the trust of his honour at my peril for the remnant. But yet, thinketh me, Lo, that if I may not declare the causes without peril, then to leave them undeclared is no obstinacy. My Lord of Canterbury taking hold upon that that I said, that I condemned not the consciences of them that sware, said unto me that it appeared well, that I did not take it for a very sure thing and a certain, that I might not lawfully swear it, but rather as a thing uncertain and doubtful. But then (said my Lord) you know for a certainty, and a thing without doubt, that you be bounden to obey your sovereign lord your king. And therefore are ye bounden to leave of the doubt of your unsure conscience in refusing the oath, and take the sure way in obeying of your prince, and swear it. Now all was it so, that in mine own mind methought myself not concluded, yet this argument seemed me suddenly so subtle, and namely with such authority coming out of so noble a prelate's mouth, that I could again answer nothing thereto but only that I thought myself I might not well do so, because that in my conscience this was one of the cases in which I was bounden that I should not obey my prince, sith that whatsoever other folk thought in the matter (whose conscience or learning I would not condemn nor take upon me to judge), yet in my conscience the truth seemed on the tother side. Wherein I had not informed my conscience neither suddenly nor slightly, but by long leisure and diligent search for the matter. And of truth if that reason may conclude, then have we a ready way to avoid all perplexities. For in whatsoever matter the doctors stand in great doubt, the king's commandment given upon whitherside he list, soyleth all the doubts. Then said my Lord of Westminster to me, that howsoever the matter seemed unto mine own mind, I had cause to fear that mine own mind was erroneous, when I see the Great Council of the realm

determine of my mind the contrary, and that therefore I ought to change my conscience. To that I
answered, that if there were no more but myself
upon my side, and the whole parliament upon the
tother, I would be sore afraid to lean to mine own
mind only against so many. But on the other side,
if it so be that in some things, for which I refuse the
oath, I have (as I think I have) upon my part as great
a Council and a greater too, I am not then bounden
to change my conscience and conform it to the Council
of one realm, against the general Council of Christendom. Upon this Master Secretary, as he that tenderly favoureth me, said and sware a great oath, that
he had sooner that his own only son (which is of
truth a goodly young gentleman, and shall I trust
come to much worship) had lost his head than that
I should thus have refused the oath. For surely the
king's highness would now conceive a great suspicion
against me, and think that the matter of the nun of
Canterbury was all contrived by my drift. To
which I said that the contrary was true and well
known. And whatsoever should mishap me, it lay
not in my power to help it without the peril of
my soul. Then did my Lord Chancellor repeat
before me my refusal unto Master Secretary, as to
him that was going unto the king's grace. And in

the rehearsing, his Lordship repeated again, that I denied not but was content to swear unto the succession. Whereunto I said, that as for that point I would be content, so that I might see my oath in that point so framed in such a manner as might stand with my conscience. Then said my Lord : Marry, Master Secretary, mark that too, that he will not swear that neither, but under some certain manner. Verily, no, my Lord, quoth I, but that I will see it made in such wise first, as I shall myself see, that I shall neither be foresworn, nor swear against my conscience. Surely as to swear to the succession I see no peril. But I thought and think it reason that to mine own oath I look well myself, and be of counsel also in the fashion, and never intended to swear for a piece, and set my hand to the whole oath. Howbeit, as help me God, as touching the whole oath I never withdrew any man from it, nor never advised any to refuse it, nor never put, nor will put, any scruple in any man's head, but leave every man to his own conscience. And me thinketh in good faith that so were it good reason that every man should leave me to mine.

LETTER II

In August, in the Year of our Lord 1534, *and in the twenty-sixth year of the Reign of King Henry the Eighth, the Lady* ALICE ALINGTON (*Wife to Sir* GILES ALINGTON, *Knight, and Daughter to Sir Thomas More's second and last Wife*) *wrote a letter to Mistress* MARGARET ROPER, *the Copy whereof here followeth.*

SISTER ROPER, with all my heart, I recommend me unto you, thanking you for all kindness. The cause of my writing at this time is, to show you that at my coming home, within two hours after, my Lord Chancellor did come to take a course at a buck in our park, the which was to my husband a great comfort, that it would please him so to do. Then when he had taken his pleasure and killed his deer, he went to Sir Thomas Barnston's to bed: where I was the next day with him at his desire, the which I could not say nay to, for methought he did bid me heartily: and most especially because I would speak to him for my father. And when I saw my time, I did desire him as humbly as I could that he would (as I have heard say that he hath been) be still good lord unto my father. First he answered me that he would be as glad to do for him as for his father, and that (he said) did appear very well when the matter of the nun was laid to his charge. And as for this other matter, he marvelled that my father is so obstinate in his own conceit, in that everybody went forth withal, save only the blind bishop and he. And in good faith (said my Lord) I am very glad that I have no learning, but in a few of Æsop's fables, of the which I shall tell you one. There was a country in the which there were almost none but fools, saving a few which were wise, and they by their wisdom knew that there should fall a great rain, the which should make all them fools, that should be fouled or wet therewith. They, seeing that, made them caves under the ground, till all the rain was past. Then they came forth, thinking to make the fools do what they list, and to rule them as they would. But the fools would none of that, but would have the rule themselves for all their craft. And when the wise men saw that they could not obtain their purpose they wished that they had been in the rain, and had defiled their clothes with them. When this tale was told my lord did laugh very merrily. Then I said to him, that for all his merry fable I did put no doubts but that he would be good lord unto my father when he saw his time. He said, I would not have your father so scrupulous of his conscience. And then he told me another fable of a Lion, an Ass and a Wolf, and of their confession. First the Lion confessed that he had devoured all the beasts he could come by. His confessor assoyled him because he was a king, and also it was his nature so to do. Then came the poor Ass, and said that he took but one straw out of his master's shoe for hunger, by the means whereof he thought that his master did take cold. His confessor could not assoil this great trespass but by and bye sent him to the bishop. Then came the Wolf and made his confession, and he was straightly commanded that he should not pass sixpence at a meal. But when the said wolf had used this diet a little while, he waxed very hungry, in so much, that on a day when he saw a cow with her calf come by him, he said to himself, I am very hungry, and fain would I eat, but that I am bound by my ghostly father. Notwithstanding that, my conscience shall judge me. And then, if that be so, then shall my conscience be thus, that the cow doth seem to me now but worth a groat. And then if the cow be but worth a groat, then is the calf but worth two pence ; so did the

wolf eat both the cow and the calf.   Now, my good
sister, hath not my lord told me two pretty fables?
In good faith they pleased me nothing, nor I wist
not what to say, for I was abashed of his answer.
And I see no better suit than to Almighty God, for
He is the comforter of all sorrows, and will not fail to
send His comfort to His servants when they have
most need.   Thus fare ye well, my own good sister.
Written the Monday after Saint Laurence, in haste,
Your Sister,
ALICE ALINGTON.

LETTER III

When Mistress ROPER *had received this Letter, she, at her next repair to her Father in the Tower, showed him this Letter. And what communication was there-upon between her Father and her, ye shall perceive by an Answer here following (as written to the Lady* ALINGTON). *But whether this answer were written by Sir* THOMAS MORE *in his Daughter* ROPER'S *name, or by herself, it is not certainly known.*

WHEN I came next unto my father after, me thought it both convenient and necessary, to show him your letter—convenient, that he might thereby see your loving labour taken for him ; necessary, that sith he might perceive thereby, that if he stand still in this scruple of his conscience, (as it is at the least wise called by many that are his friends and wife) all his friends that seem most able to do him good, either shall finally forsake him, or peradventure not be able indeed to do him any good at all. And for these causes, at my next being with him after your letter received, when I had a while talked with him, first of his diseases both in his breast of old, and his reins now, by reason of gravel and stone, and of the cramp also that divers nights grippeth him in his legs, and that I found by his words that they were not much increased, but continued after their manner that they did before, sometime very sore and sometime little grief, and that at that time I found him out of pain, and as one in his case might, meetly well-minded, after our seven psalms and the litany said, to sit and talk and be merry, beginning first with other things, of the good comfort of my mother, and the good order of my brother, and all my sisters, disposing themselves every day more and more to set little by the world, and draw more and more to God, and that his household, his neighbours, and other good friends abroad, diligently remembered him in their prayers, I added unto this ; I pray God, good father, that their prayers, and ours, and your own therewith, may purchase of God the grace that you may in this great matter (for which you stand in this trouble, and for your trouble all we also that love you) take such a way by time, as standing with the pleasure of God, may content and please the king, whom ye have always founden so singularly gracious unto you, that if ye should stiffly refuse to do the thing that were his pleasure, which, God not displeased, you might do, (as many great, wise, and well-learned men, say that in this thing you may), it would both be a great blot in your worship in every wise man's opinion, and as myself have heard some say (such as yourself have always taken for well-learned and good) a peril unto your soul also. But as for that point (father) will I not be bold to dispute upon, since I trust in God, and your good mind, that ye will look surely thereto. And your learning I know for such, that I wot well you can. But one thing is there, which I and other your friends find and perceive abroad, which, but if it be showed you, you may peradventure to your great peril mistake, and hope for less harm (for as for good I wot well in this world of this matter ye look for none) than, I sore fear me, shall be likely to fall to you. For I assure you, father, I have received a letter of late from my sister *Alington*, by which I see well, that if ye change not your mind, you are likely to lose all those friends that are able to do you any good. Or if ye lese not their good wills, you shall at the least wise lese the effect thereof, for any good that they shall be able to do you. With this my father smiled upon me and said : What, mistress Eve, (as I called you when you came first), hath my daughter

Alington played the serpent with you, and with a letter set you awork to come tempt your father again, and for the favour that you bear him, labour to make him swear against his conscience, and so send him to the devil ? And after that, he looked sadly again, and earnestly said unto me, daughter *Margaret*, we two have talked of this thing ofter than twice or thrice. And the same tale, in effect, that you tell me now therein, and the same fear too, have you twice told me before, and I have twice answered you too, that in this matter if it were possible for me to do the thing that might content the king's grace, and God therewith not offended, then hath no man taken this oath already more gladly than I would do ; as he that reckoneth himself more deeply bounden unto the king's highness, for his most singular bounty, many ways showed and declared, than any of them all beside. But sith standing my conscience I can in no wise do it, and that for the instruction of my conscience in the matter, I have not slightly looked, but by many years istudied, and advisedly considered, and never could yet see nor hear that thing, nor I think I never shall, that could induce mine own mind to think otherwise than I do, I have no manner remedy, but God hath given me to that strait, that either I must deadly displease Him, or abide any worldly harm that

He shall for mine other sins, under name of this thing, suffer to fall upon me. Whereof (as I before this have told you too) I have, ere I came here, not left unbethought nor unconsidered, the very most and the uttermost that can by possibility fall. And albeit that I know mine own frailty full well, and the natural faintness of mine own heart, yet if I had not trusted that God should give me strength rather to endure all things, than offend Him by swearing ungodly against mine own conscience, you may be very sure I would not have come here. And sith I look, in this matter, but only unto God, it maketh me little matter, though men call it as it please them, and say it is no conscience, but a foolish scruple. At this word I took a good occasion, and said unto him thus: In good faith, father, for my part, I neither do, nor it cannot become me, either to mistrust your good mind or your learning. But because you speak of that that some call it but a scruple, I assure you you shall see by my sister's letter, that one, of the greatest estates in this realm, and a man learned too, and (as I dare say yourself shall think when you know him, and as you have already right effectually proved him) your tender friend and very special good lord, accounteth your conscience in this matter, for a right simple scruple. And you may be sure he saith it of good mind, and hath no

121

little cause. For he saith, that where you say your conscience moveth you to this, all the nobles of this realm, and almost all other men too, go boldly forth with the contrary, and stick not thereat, save only yourself and one other man : whom though he be right good, and very well learned too, yet would I ween few that love you, give you the counsel against all other men to lean to his mind alone. And with this word I took him your letter, that he might see that my words were not feigned, but spoken of his mouth whom he much loveth and esteemeth highly. Thereupon he read over your letter. And when he came to the end, he began it afresh and read over again. And in the reading he made no manner haste, but advised it leisurely, and pointed every word. And after that he paused, and then thus he said. Forsooth, daughter *Margaret*, I find my daughter *Alington* such as I have ever found her, and I trust ever shall, as naturally minding me as you that are mine own. Howbeit, her take I verily for mine own too, since I have married her mother, and brought up her of a child, as I have brought up you, in other things and in learning both, wherein I thank God she findeth now some fruit, and bringeth her own up very virtuously and well. Whereof God, I thank Him, hath sent her good store, our Lord preserve them and send her much joy of them, and my good son her gentle husband too, and have mercy on the soul of mine other good son, her first : I am daily bedesman (and so write her) for them all. In this matter she has used herself like herself, wisely, and like a very daughter toward me ; and in the end of her letter, giveth as good counsel as any man (that wit hath) would wish, God give me grace to follow it, and God reward her for it. Now, daughter *Margaret,* as for my lord, I not only think, but have also found it, that he is undoubtedly my singular good lord. And in mine other business, concerning the sely nun, as my cause was good and clear, so was he my good lord therein, and Mr. Secretary my good master too. For which I shall never cease to be faithful bedesman for them both, and daily do I, by my troth, pray for them as I pray for myself. And whensoever it should happen (which I trust in God shall never happen) that I be found other than a true man to my prince, let them never favour me, neither of them both, nor of truth no more it could become them so to do. But in this matter, *Megg,* to tell the truth between thee and me, my lord's Æsop's fables do not greatly move me. But as his wisdom, for his pastime, told them merely to my one daughter, so shall I, for my pastime, answer them to

123

thee, *Megg*, that art mine other. The first fable, of
the rain that washed away all their wits that stood
abroad when it fell, I have heard oft ere this : it
was a tale so often told among the king's Council by
my Lord Cardinal, when his grace was chancellor,
that I cannot lightly forget it. For of truth in times
past, when variance began to fall between the
Emperor and the French king, in such wise that
they were likely, and did indeed, fall together at war,
and that there were in the Council here sometimes
sundry opinions, in which some were of the mind
that they thought it wisdom, that we should sit still
and let them alone : but evermore against that way,
my lord used this fable of those wise men, that
because they would not be washed with the rain that
should make all the people fools, went themselves in
caves and hid them under the ground. But when
the rain had once made all the remnant fools, and
that they came out of their caves and would utter
their wisdom, the fools agreed together against them,
and there all to bet them. And so said his grace,
that if we would be so wise that we would sit in
peace while the fools fought, they would not fail
after to make peace and agree, and fall at length all
upon us. I will not dispute upon his grace's counsel, and I trust we never made war, but as reason

would. But yet this fable, for his part, did in his days help the king and the realm to spend many a fair penny. But that grace is passed, and his grace is gone, our Lord assoil his soul. And, therefore, shall I now come to this Æsop's fable, as my Lord full merrily laid it forth for me. If those wise men, *Megg*, when the rain was gone at their coming abroad, where they found all men fools, wished themselves fools too, because they could not rule them, then seemeth it that the foolish rain was so sore a shower, that even through the ground it sank into their caves, and poured down upon their heads, and wet them to the skin, and made them more noddies than them that stood abroad. For if they had had any wit, they might well see, that though they had been fools too, that thing would not have sufficed to make them the rulers over the other fools, no more than the tother fools over them : and of so many fools all might not be rulers. Now when they longed so sore to bear a rule among fools, that so they so might, they would be glad to lese their wit and be fools too, the foolish rain had washed them meetly well. Howbeit to say the truth, before the rain came, if they thought that all the remnant should turn into fools, then either were so foolish that they would, or so mad to think that they should, so few rule so many fools, and had not so much wit, as to consider that there are none so unruly as they that lack wit and are fools, then were these wise men stark fools before the rain came. Howbeit, daughter *Roper*, whom my Lord here taketh for the wise men, and whom he meaneth to be fools, I cannot very well guess, I cannot read well such riddles. For as *Davus* saith in Terence : *Non sum Œdipus*. I may say you wot well : *Non sum Œdipus, sed Morus*, which name of mine what it signifieth in Greek, I need not tell you. But I trust my Lord reckoneth me among the fools, and so reckoneth I myself, as my name is in Greek. And I find, I thank God, causes not a few, wherefore I so should in every deed. But surely, among those that long to be rulers, God and mine own conscience clearly knoweth, that no man may truly number and reckon me. And I ween each other man's conscience can tell himself the same, since it is so well known that of the king's great goodness, I was one of the greatest rulers in this noble realm, and that at mine own great labour by his great goodness discharged. But whomsoever my lord mean for the wise men, and whomsoever his lordship take for the fools, and whosoever long for the rule, and whosoever long for none, I beseech our Lord make us all so wise as that we may every man here so wisely rule ourself, in this time of tears, this vale of misery, this simple wretched world (in which, as Boece saith, one man to be proud that he beareth rule over other men, is much like as one mouse would be proud to bear a rule over other mice in a barn), God, I say, give us the grace so wisely to rule ourself here, that when we shall hence in haste to meet the great spouse, we be not taken sleepers, and for lack of light in our lamps, shut out of heaven among the five foolish virgins. The second fable, *Marget*, seemeth not to be Æsop's. For by that the matter goeth all upon confession, it seemeth to be feigned since Christendom began. For in Greece, before Christ's days, they used not confession no more the men then, than the beasts now. And Æsop was a Greek, and died long ere Christ was born. But what ? who made it, maketh but little matter. Nor I envy not that Æsop hath the name. But surely it is somewhat too subtle for me. For when his lordship understandeth by the lion, and the wolf, which both twain confessed themselves of ravin and devouring of all that came to their hands, and the t'one enlarged his conscience at his pleasure in the construction of his penance, nor whom by the good discreet confessor that enjoined the t'one a little penance, and the tother none at all, and sent the poor ass to the bishop, of all these things can I nothing tell. But by the foolish scrupulous ass, that had so sore a conscience for the taking of a straw for hunger out of his master's shoe, my lord's other words of my scruple declare, that his lordship merely meant that by me : signifying (as it seemeth by that similitude), that of oversight and folly, my scrupulous conscience taketh for a great perilous thing toward my soul, if I should swear this oath, which thing, as his lordship thinketh, were indeed but a trifle. And I suppose well, *Margaret*, as you told me right now, that so thinketh many more beside, as well spiritual as temporal, and that even of those, that for their learning and their virtue, myself not a little esteemed. And yet albeit that I suppose this to be true, yet believe I not even very surely, that every man so thinketh that so saith. But though they did, daughter, that would not make much to me, not though I should see my Lord of Rochester say the same, and swear the oath himself before me too. For whereas you told me right now, that such as love me, would not advise me, that against all other men, I should lean into his mind alone, verily, daughter, no more I do. For albeit that of very truth, I have him in that reverent esti-mation, that I reckon in this realm no one man, in wisdom, learning, and long approved virtue together, meet to be matched and compared with him, yet that in this matter I was not led by him, very well and plain appeareth, both in that I refused the oath before it was offered him, and in that also that his lordship was content to have sworn of that oath (as I perceived since by you when you moved me to the same) either somewhat more, or in some other manner than ever I minded to do. Verily, daughter, I never intend (God being my good Lord) to pin my soul at another man's back, not even the best man that I know this day living : for I know not whither he may hap to carry it. There is no man living, of whom while he liveth, I may make myself sure. Some may do for favour, and some may do for fear, and so might they carry my soul a wrong way. And some might hap to frame himself a conscience, and think that while he did it for fear, God would forgive it. And some may peradventure think that they will repent, and be shriven thereof, and that so shall God remit it them. And some may be peradventure of the mind, that if they say one thing and think the while the contrary, God more regardeth their heart than their tongue, and that therefore their oath goeth upon that they think, and not upon that they say : as a woman reasoned once,

I trow, daughter, you were by. But in good faith, *Marget*, I can use no such ways in so great a matter : but like as if mine own conscience served me, I would not let to do it though other men refused, so though others refuse it not, I dare not do it, mine own conscience standing against it. If I had (as I told you) looked but lightly for the matter, I should have cause to fear. But now have I so looked for it, and so long, that I purpose at the least wise to have no less regard unto my soul, than at once a poor honest man of the country, that was called Company. And with this he told me a tale, I ween I can scant tell it you again, because it hangeth upon some terms and ceremonies of the law. But as far as I can call to mind, my father's tale was this, that there is a court belonging, of course, unto every fair, to do justice in such things as happen within the same. This court hath a pretty fond name, but I cannot happen on it : but it beginneth with a "Pie," and the remnant goeth much like the name of a knight that I have known, I wis, and I trow you too, for he hath been at my father's oft ere this, at such time as you were there, a meetly tall black man, his name was Sir William Pounder. But, tut ! let the name of the court for this once, or call it if ye will a "court of Pie Sir-William-Pounder." But this was the matter, lo, that upon a time, at such a court holden at Bartholomew Fair, there was an escheator of London that had arrested a man that was outlawed, and had seized his goods that he had brought into the fair, tolling him out of the fair by a train. The man that was arrested, and his goods seized, was a northern man, which, by his friends, made the escheator within the Fair to be arrested upon an action, I wot ne'er what, and so was he brought before the judge, of the court of " Pie Sir-William-Pounder." And at the last that that matter came to a certain ceremony to be tried by a quest of twelve men, a jury, as I remember they called it, or else a perjury. Now had the clothman, by friendship of the officers, founden the means to have all the quest almost made of the northern men, such as had their booths there standing in the Fair. Now was it come to the last day in the afternoon, and the twelve men had heard both the parties, and their counsel tell their tales at the bar, and were from the bar had into a place, to talk, and common, and agree upon their sentence. Nay, let me speak better in my terms yet, I trow the judge giveth the sentence, and the quests' tale is called a verdict. They were scant come in together, but the northern men were agreed, and in effect all the tother too, to cast our London escheator. They thought there needed no more to prove that he did wrong, than even the name of his bare office alone. But then was there among them, as the devil would, this honest man of another quarter, that was called Company. And because the fellow seemed but a fool, and sat still and said nothing, they made no reckoning of him, but said We be agreed now, come let us go and give our verdict. Then when the poor fellow saw that they made such haste, and his mind nothing gave him that way that theirs did (if their minds gave them that way that they said), he prayed them to tarry and talk upon that matter, and tell him such reason therein, that he might think as they did : and when he so should do, he would be glad to say with them, or else, he said, they must pardon him. For sith he had a soul of his own to keep, as they had, he must say as he thought for his, as they must for theirs. When they heard this they were half angry with him. What, good fellow, (quoth one of the northern men) where wonnest thou ? Be not we eleven here, and thou be but one alone, and all we agreed ? Whereto shouldst thou stick ? What is thy name, good fellow ? Masters (quoth he), my name is called Company. Company, quoth they, now by thy troth, good fellow, play then the good companion, come thereon forth with us, and pass even for good

company.   Would God, good masters, quoth the
man again, that there lay no more weight thereon.
But now when we shall hence and come before God,
and that He shall send you to heaven for doing
according to your conscience, and me to the devil for
doing against mine, in passing at your request here
for good company now, by God, Master Dickenson,
(that was one of the northern men's names), if I shall
then say to all you again, Masters, I went once for
good company with you, which is the cause I go now
to hell, play you the good fellows now again with
me, as I went then for good company with you, so
some of you go now for good company with me.
Would ye go, Master Dickenson ? Nay, nay, by Our
Lady, nor never one of you all.   And therefore must
ye pardon me, from passing as you pass, but if I
thought in that matter as you do, I dare not in such
a matter pass for good company.   For the passage of
my poor soul passeth all good company.   And when
my father had told me this tale, then said he further
thus : I pray thee now, good *Margaret*, tell me this,
wouldst thou wish thy poor father, being at the least
wise somewhat learned, less to regard the peril of his
soul, than did there that honest unlearned man ? I
meddle not (you wot well) with the conscience of
any man that hath sworn : nor I take not upon me

to be their judge.   But now if they do well, and
that their conscience grudge them not, if I, with
my conscience to the contrary, should for good
company pass on with them, and swear as they do,
when all our souls hereafter shall pass out of this
world, and stand in judgment at the bar before
the High Judge, if He judge them to heaven, and
me to the devil, because I did as they did, not
thinking as they thought, if I should then say
(as the good man Company said) : Mine old good
lords and friends, naming such a lord and such,
yea, and some bishops, peradventure of such as I love
best, I sware because you sware, and went that way
that you went, do likewise for me now, let me not
go alone; if there be any good fellowship with you,
some of you come with me : by my troth, *Margaret*,
I may say to thee in secret counsel, here between us
twain, (but let it go no further I beseech thee
heartily,) I find the friendship of this wretched world
so fickle, that for any thing that I could treat or pray,
that would for good fellowship go to to the devil
with me, among them all, I ween, should not I find
one.   And then, by God, *Margaret*, if you think so
too, best it is, I suppose, that for any respect of them
all, were they twice as many more as they be, I have
myself a respect to mine own soul.   Surely, father,

quoth I, without any scruple at all, you may be bold, I dare say, for to swear that. But, father, they that think you should not refuse to swear the thing, that you see so many, so good men and so well learned, swear before you, mean not that you should swear to bear them fellowship, nor to pass with them for good company : but that the credence that you may with reason give to their persons for their aforesaid qualities, should well move you to think the oath such of itself, as every man may well swear without peril of their soul, if their own private conscience to the contrary be not the lest : and that ye well ought, and have good cause, to change your own conscience, in confirming your own conscience to the conscience of so many other, namely, being such as you know they be. And sith it is also by a law made by the parliament commanded, they think that you be, upon the peril of your soul, bounden to change and reform your conscience, and confirm your own as I said unto other mens'. Marry, *Margaret*, (quoth my father again) for the part that you play, you play it not much amiss. But *Margaret*, first, as for the law of the land, though every man being born and inhabiting therein is bounden to the keeping in every case upon some temporal pain, and in many cases upon pain of God's displeasure too, yet is there no man bounden to swear that every law is well made, nor bounden upon the pain of God's displeasure to perform any such point of the law as were indeed unlawful. Of which manner kind, that there may such hap to be, made in any part of Christendom, I suppose no man doubteth the general Council of the whole body of Christendom evermore in that point except: which, though it may make some things better than other, and some things may grow to that point, that by another law they may need to be reformed, yet to institute any thing in such wise to God's displeasure, as at the making might not lawfully be performed, the spirit of God that governeth His church, never had yet suffered, nor never hereafter shall, His whole Catholic Church lawfully gathered together in a general Council, as Christ hath made plain promises in Scripture. Now if it so hap, that in any particular part of Christendom there be a law made, that be such, as for some part thereof some men think that the law of God cannot bear it, and some other think yes, the thing being in such manner in question, that thorough divers quarters of Christendom, some that are good men and cunning, both of our own days, and before our days, think some one way, and some other of like learning and goodness think the contrary, in this case he that thinketh against the law,

136

neither may swear that law lawfully was made, standing his own conscience to the contrary, nor is bounden upon pain of God's displeasure to change his own conscience therein, for any particular law made anywhere, other than by the general counsel, or by a general faith grown by the working of God universally through all Christian nations ; nor other authority than one of these twain (except special revelation and express commandment of God) sith the contrary opinions of good men and well learned, as I put you the case, made the understanding of the Scriptures doubtful, I can see none that lawfully may command and compel any man to change his own opinion, and to translate his own conscience from the t'one side to the tother. For an ensample of some such manner things, I have I trow before this time told you, that whether our blessed lady were conceived in original sin or not, was sometime in great question among the great learned men of Christendom. And whether it be yet decided and determined by any general Council, I remember not. But this I remember well, that notwithstanding that the feast of her conception was then celebrate in the church (at the leastwise in divers provinces) yet was holy S. Bernard, which, as his manifold books made in the laud and praise of our lady do declare, was of as devout affection toward all things sounding toward her commendation, that he thought might well be verified or suffered, as any man was living; yet, I say, was that holy devout man, against that part of her praise, as appeareth well by an epistle of his, wherein he right sore and with great reason argueth there against, and approveth not the institution of that feast neither. Nor he was not of this mind alone, but many other well learned men with him, and right holy men too. Now was there on the tother side, the blessed holy bishop Saint Anselm, and he not alone neither, but many well learned and very virtuous also with him. And they be both twain holy saints in heaven, and many more that were on either side. Nor neither part was there bounden to change their opinion, for the tother, nor for any provincial Council either. But like as after the determination of a well assembled general Council, every man had been bound to give credence that way, and confirm their own conscience to the determination of the Council generally, and then all they that held the contrary before, were for that holding out of blame, so if before such decision a man had against his own conscience, sworn to maintain and defend the other side, he had not failed to offend God very sore. But marry, if on the t'other side a man would in a matter take away by

138

himself upon his own mind alone, or with some few, or with never so many, against an evident truth appearing by the common faith of Christendom, this conscience is very damnable. Yea, or if it be not even fully so plain and evident, yet if he see but himself with far the fewer part, think the t'one way, against far the more part of as well learned and as good, as those are that affirm the thing that he thinketh, thinking and affirming the contrary, and that of such folk as he has no reasonable cause wherefore he should not in that matter suppose, that those which say they think against his mind, affirm the thing that they say, for no other cause but for that they so think indeed, this is of very truth a very good occasion to move him, and yet not to compel him, to conform his mind and conscience unto theirs. But *Margaret*, for what causes I refuse the oath, that thing (as I have often told you) I will never show you, neither you nor nobody else, except the king's highness should like to command me. Which if his grace did, I have ere this told you, therein how obediently I have said. But surely, daughter, I have refused it, and do, for more causes than one. And for what causes soever I refuse it, this am I sure, that it is well known, that of them that have sworn it, some of the best learned before the oath given them, said and plain affirmed the contrary, of some such things as they have now sworn in the oath, and that upon their truth and their learning then, and that not in haste nor suddenly, but often and after great diligence done to seek and find out the truth. That might be, father, (quoth I), and yet since they might see more. I will not (quoth he) dispute, daughter *Margaret*, against that, nor misjudge any other man's conscience, which lieth in their own heart far out of my sight. But this will I say, that I never heard myself the cause of their change, by any new further thing founden of authority, than as far as I perceive they had looked on, and as I suppose, very well weighed before. Now of the self same things that they saw before, seem some otherwise unto them now than they did before, I am for their sakes the gladder a great deal. But anything that ever I saw before, yet at this day to me they seem but as they did. And therefore, though they may do otherwise than they might, yet, daughter, I may not. As for such things as some men would haply say, that I might with reason the less regard their change, for any sample of them to be taken to the change of my conscience, because that the keeping of the prince's pleasure, and the avoiding of his indignation, the fear of the losing of their worldly substance with regard unto the discomfort of their kindred and their friends, might hap make some men either swear otherwise than they think, or frame their conscience afresh to think otherwise than they thought, any such opinion as this is, will I not conceive of them. I have better hope of their goodness, than to think of them so. For if such things should have turned them, the same things had been likely to make me do the same : for in good faith, I knew few so faint-hearted as myself. Therefore will I, *Margaret*, by my will, think no worse of other folk in the thing that I know not, than I find in myself. But as I know well mine only conscience causeth me to refuse the oath, so will I trust in God, that according to their conscience they have received it and sworn. But whereas you think, *Marget*, that they be so many, more than there are on the tother side that think in this thing as I think, surely for your own comfort that ye shall not take thought, thinking that your father casteth himself away so like a fool, that he would jeopardy the loss of his substance and peradventure his body, without any cause why he so should for peril of his soul, but rather his soul in peril thereby too, to this shall I say to thee, *Marget*, that in some of my causes I nothing doubt at all, but that though not in this realm, yet in Christendom about, of those well learned men and virtuous, that are yet alive, they be not the fewer part

that are of my mind. Besides that, that it were ye
wot well possible, that some men in this realm, too,
think not so clear the contrary, as by the oath received
they have sworn to say. Now thus far forth I say for
them, that are yet alive. But go we now to them
that are dead before, and that are, I trust, in heaven, I
am sure that it is not the fewer part of them, that all
the time while they lived, thought in some of the
things that way that I think now. I am also,
Margaret, of this thing sure enough, that if those holy
doctors and saints which to be with God in heaven
long ago no good Christian man doubteth, whose
books yet at this day remain here in men's
hands, there thought in some such things as
I think now. I say not that they thought all so,
but surely such and so many as will well appear by
their writing that I pray God give me the grace that
my soul may follow theirs. And yet I show you not
all, *Marget*, that I have for myself in that sure discharge
of my conscience. But for the conclusion, daughter
Margaret, of all this matter, as I have often told you,
I take not upon me neither to define nor dispute in
these matters, nor I rebuke not nor impugn any
other man's deed, nor I never wrote, nor so much as
spake in any company, any word of reproach in anything that the parliament had passed, nor I meddle

not with the conscience of any other man, that either thinketh, or saith he thinketh, contrary unto mine. But as concerning mine own self, for thy comfort shall I say, daughter, to thee, that mine own conscience in this matter (I damn none other man's) is such, as may well stand with mine own salvation ; thereof am I, *Megg*, as sure, as that God is in heaven. And therefore as for all the remnant, goods, lands, and life both (if the chance should so fortune) sith this conscience is sure for me, I verily trust in God, He shall rather strengthen me to bear the loss, than against this conscience to swear and put my soul in peril, sith all the causes that I perceive move other men to the contrary, seem not such unto me, as in my conscience make any change. When he saw me sit with this, very sad as I promise you, Sister, my heart was full heavy for the peril of his person, nay, for in faith I fear not his soul, he smiled upon me and said : how now, daughter *Marget?* What how, Mother Eve ? Where is your mind now ? Sit not musing with some serpent in your breast, upon some new persuasion, to offer father *Adam* the apple once again. In good faith, father (quoth I), I can no further go, but am (as I trow *Cressida* saith in Chaucer) come to *Dulcarnon*, even at my wits' end. For sith the ensample of so many wise men cannot in this matter move you, I see not what to say more, but if I should look to persuade you with the reason that Master Harry Pattenson made. For he met one day one of our men, and when he had asked where you were, and heard that you were in the Tower still, he waxed even angry with you and said : Why, what aileth him that he will not swear ? Wherefore should he stick to swear ? I have sworn the oath myself. And so I can in good faith go now no further neither, after so many wise men, whom ye take for no ensample, but if I should say, like Master Harry : Why should you refuse to swear, father ? for I have sworn myself.[1] At this he laughed and said : That word was like Eve too, for she offered Adam no worse fruit than she had eaten herself. But yet, father (quoth I), by my troth, I fear me very sore, that this matter will bring you in marvellous heavy trouble. You know well that as I showed you, Master Secretary sent you word as your very friend, to remember that the parliament lasteth yet. *Margaret*, quoth my father, I thank him right heartily. But as I showed you then again, I left not this gear unthought on. And albeit I know well that if they would make a law to do me any harm that law could never be

---

[1] She took the oath with this exception, as far as it would stand with the law of God.

lawful, but that God shall I trust keep me in that grace that concerning my duty to my prince, no man shall do me hurt, but if he do me wrong (and then as I told you, this is like a riddle, a case in which a man may lese his head and have no harm) ; and notwithstanding, also, that I have good hope that God shall never suffer so good and wise a prince in such wise to requite the long service of his true faithful servant, yet sith there is nothing impossible to fall, I forgat not in this matter the counsel of Christ in the Gospel, that ere I should begin to build this castle for the safeguard of mine own soul, I should sit and reckon what the charge would be. I counted, *Marget*, full surely many a restless night, while my wife slept, and weened I had slept too, what peril were possible for to fall to me, so far forth that I am sure there can come none above. And in devising, daughter, thereupon, I had a full heavy heart. But yet I thank our Lord for all that, I never thought to change, though the very uttermost should hap me that my fear ran upon. No, father, (quoth I,) it is not like to think upon a thing that may be, and to see a thing that shall be, as ye should (our Lord save you), if the chance should so fortune. And then should you peradventure think that you think not now, yet then peradventure it would be too late. Too late, daughter (quoth my father) *Margaret*? I beseech our Lord, that if ever I make such a change it may be too late indeed. For well I wot the change cannot be good for my soul, that change I say that should grow but by fear. And therefore I pray God that in this world I never have good of such change. For so much as I take harm here, I shall have at the leastwise the less therefore when I am hence. And if it so were that I wist well now, that I should faint and fall, and for fear swear hereafter, yet would I wish to take harm by the refusing first, for so should I have the better hope for grace to rise again. And albeit (*Marget*) that I wot well my lewdness hath been such : that I know myself well worthy that God should let me slip, yet can I not but trust in His merciful goodness, that as His grace hath strengthened me hitherto, and made me content in my heart, to lese good, land, and life too, rather than swear against my conscience, and hath also put in the king toward me, that good and gracious mind, that as yet he hath taken from me nothing but my liberty (wherewith, as help me God), his grace hath done me so great good by the spiritual profit that I trust I take thereby, that among all his great benefits heaped upon me so thick, I reckon upon my faith my imprisonment even the very chief ; I cannot, I say, therefore, mistrust the grace of God, but that either He shall conserve and keep the king in that gracious mind still, to do me none hurt, or else if His pleasure be, that for mine other sins I shall suffer in such a cause in sight as I shall not deserve, His grace shall give me that strength to take it patiently, and peradventure somewhat gladly too, whereby His High Goodness shall (by the merits of His bitter passion joined thereunto, and far surmounting in merit for me, all that I can suffer myself) make it serve for release of my pain in purgatory, and over that for increase of some reward in heaven. Mistrust Him, *Megg*, will I not, though I feel me faint. Yea, and though I should feel my fear even at point to overthrow me too, yet shall I remember how Saint Peter with a blast of wind began to sink for his faint faith, and shall do as he did, call upon Christ and pray Him to help. And then I trust He shall set His holy hand unto me, and in the stormy seas, hold me up from drowning. Yea, and if He suffer me to play Saint Peter further, and to fall full to the ground, and swear and forswear too (which our Lord for His tender passion keep me from, and let me lese if it so fall, and never win thereby) ; yet after shall I trust that His goodness shall cast upon me His tender piteous eye, as He did upon Saint Peter, and make me stand up again and confess the truth of my

147

conscience afresh, and abide the shame and the harm here of mine own fault. And finally, *Marget*, this wot I very well, that without my fault He will not let me be lost. I shall therefore with good hope commit myself wholly to Him. And if He suffer me for my faults to perish, yet shall I then serve for a praise of His justice. But in good faith, *Meg*, I trust that His tender pity shall keep my poor soul safe, and make me commend His mercy. And therefore, mine own good daughter, never trouble thy mind for anything that ever shall hap me in this world. Nothing can come but that that God will. And I make me very sure that whatsoever that be, seem it never so bad in sight, it shall indeed be the best. And with this, my good child, I pray you heartily, be you and all your sisters, and my sons too, comfortable and serviceable to your good mother my wife. And of your good husbands' minds I have no manner doubt. Commend me to them all, and to my good daughter *Alington*, and to all my other friends, sisters, nieces, nephews, and allies, and unto all our servants, man, woman, and child, and all my good neighbours, and our acquaintance abroad. And I right heartily pray both you and them, to serve God, and be merry and rejoice in Him. And if anything hap me that you would be loth, pray to God for me, but trouble not yourself: as I shall full heartily pray for us all, that we may meet together once in heaven, where we shall make merry for ever, and never have trouble hereafter.

LETTER IV

Another Letter of Sir THOMAS MORE *to his daughter,* Mrs. MARGARET ROPER, *written with a coal.*

MINE own good daughter, our Lord be thanked, I am in good health of body, and in good quiet of mind ; and of worldly things I no more desire than I have. I beseech Him make you all merry in the hope of heaven. And such things as I somewhat longed to talk with you all, concerning the world to come, our Lord put them into your minds, as I trust He doth, and better too, by His Holy Spirit ; Who bless you and preserve you all. Written with a coal by your tender loving father, who in his poor prayers forgetteth none of you all, nor your babes, nor your nurses, nor your good husbands, nor your good husbands' shrewd wives, nor your father's shrewd wife neither, nor our other friends. And thus fare ye heartily well for lack of paper.

THOMAS MORE, KNIGHT.

LETTER V

A third letter of Sir THOMAS MORE'S *to his daughter,* Mrs. MARGARET ROPER, *in answer to a Letter of hers to him persuading him to take the Oath of Succession.*

Our Lord bless you.

IF I had not been, my dearly beloved daughter, at a firm and fast point, I trust, in God's great mercy this good great while before, your lamentable letter had not a little abashed me, surely far above all other things, of which I hear divers times not a few terrible toward me. But surely they all touched me never so near, nor were so grievous unto me, as to see you, my well-beloved child, in such vehement piteous manner, labour to persuade unto me the thing wherein I have, of pure necessity for respect unto mine own soul, so often given you so precise answer before. Wherein as touching the points of your letter, I can make none answer. For I doubt not but you well remember, that the matters which move my conscience (without declaration whereof I can nothing touch the points), I have sundry times showed you that I will disclose them to no man. And, therefore, daughter Margaret, I can in this thing no further, but like as you labour me again to follow your mind, to desire and pray you both again, to leave off such labour, and with my former answers to hold yourself content. A deadly grief unto me, and much more deadly than to hear of mine own death, (for the fear thereof, I thank our Lord, the fear of hell, the hope of heaven, and the passion of Christ daily more and more assuage) is, that I perceive my good son your husband, and you my good daughter, and my good wife, and mine other good children and innocent friends, in great displeasure and danger of great harm thereby. The let whereof, while it lieth not in my hand, I can no further but commit all to God. *Nam in manu dei* (saith the Scripture) *cor regis est, et sicut divisiones aquarum quocunque voluerit impellit illud.* Whose high goodness I most humbly beseech to incline the noble heart of the king's highness to the tender favour of you all, and to favour me no better than God and myself know that my faithful heart toward him and my daily prayer for him do deserve. For surely if his highness might inwardly see my true mind such as God knoweth it is, it would, I trust, soon assuage his high displeasure. Which while I can in this world never in such wise shew, but that his Grace may be persuaded to believe the contrary of me, I can no further go, but put all in the hands of Him for fear of Whose displeasure, for the safeguard of my soul stirred by mine own conscience, (without insectation, or reproach laying to any other man's) I suffer and endure this trouble. Out of which I beseech Him to bring me, when His will shall be, into His endless bliss of Heaven, and in the meanwhile, give me grace and you both, in all our agonies and troubles, devoutly to resort prostrate unto the remembrance of that bitter agony, which our Saviour suffered before His passion at the Mount. And if we diligently so do, I verily trust we shall find therein great comfort and consolation. And thus, my dear daughter, the blessed spirit of Christ, for His tender mercy, govern and guide you all, to His pleasure and your weal and comforts, both body and soul.

Your tender loving Father,
THOMAS MORE, Knight.

LETTER VI

To this last Letter Mistress MARGARET ROPER *wrote an answer and sent it to Sir* THOMAS MORE *her father, the copy whereof here followeth.*

MINE own good father ; it is to me no little comfort, sith I cannot talk with you by such means as I
would, at the least way to delight myself among in
this bitter time of your absence, by such means as
I may, by as often writing to you as shall be
expedient, and by reading again and again your most
fruitful and delectable letter, the faithful messenger of
your very virtuous and ghostly mind, rid from all
corrupt love of worldly things, and fast knit only in
the love of God and desire of Heaven, as becometh a
very true worshipper and a faithful servant of God,
which I doubt not, good father, holdeth His holy

hand over you, and shall (as He hath) preserve you both body and soul ; (*ut sit mens sana in corpore sano*) and namely now, when you have abjected all earthly consolations, and resigned yourself willingly, gladly, and fully for His love to His holy protection. Father, what think you hath been our comfort since your departing from us ? Surely the experience we have had of your life past and godly conversation and wholesome counsel, and virtuous example, and a surety not only of the continuance of that same, but also a great increase, by the goodness of our Lord, to the great rest and gladness of your heart, devoid of all earthly dregs and garnished with the noble vesture of heavenly virtues, a pleasant palace for the holy spirit of God to rest in, Who defend you (as I doubt not, good father, but of His goodness He will) from all trouble of mind and of body, and give me your most loving obedient daughter and handmaid, and all us your children and friends, to follow that we praise in you, and to our only comfort remember and commune together of you, that we may in conclusion meet with you, mine own dear father, in the bliss of Heaven, to which our most merciful Lord hath bought us with His precious blood.

Your own most loving obedient daughter and bedeswoman Margaret Roper, which desireth above all worldly things to be in John a Wood's stead to do you some service. But we live in hope that we shall shortly receive you again. I pray God heartily we may, if it be His holy will.

LETTER VII

.

A Letter written and sent by Sir THOMAS MORE *to his daughter Mistress* ROPER, *written the second or third day of May, in the Year of our Lord,* 1535, *and in the* 27*th Year of the Reign of King* HENRY VIII.

Our Lord bless you.

MY dearly beloved daughter, I doubt not but by the reason of the King's councillors resorting hither in this time, in which (our Lord be their comfort) these fathers of the Charterhouse and Master Reynolds of Sion be now judged to death for treason (whose matters and causes I know not) may hap to put you in trouble and fear of mind concerning me being here prisoner, specially for that it is not unlikely that you have heard that I was brought also before the council here myself, I have thought it necessary to advertise you of the very truth, to the end that you should neither conceive more hope than the matter giveth, lest upon another turn it might aggrieve your heaviness : nor more grief and fear than the matter giveth on the tother side. Wherefore shortly ye shall understand that on Friday, the last day of April in the afternoon, Master Lieutenant came in here unto me, and showed me that Master Secretary would speak with me, whereupon I shifted my gown, and went out with Master Lieutenant into the gallery to him, where I met many, some known and some unknown, in the way. And in conclusion coming into the chamber where his Mastership sat with Master Attorney, Master Solicitor, Master Bedell, and Master Doctor Tregonwell, I was offered to sit down with them, which in no wise I would. Whereupon Master Secretary showed unto me, that he doubted not, but that I had, by such friends as hither had resorted to me, seen the new statutes made at the last sitting of the parliament. Whereunto I answered : Yea, verily. Howbeit forasmuch as, being here, I have no conversation with any people, I thought it little need for me to bestow much time upon them, and therefore I redelivered the book shortly, and the effect of the statutes I never marked or studied to put in remembrance. Then he asked me whether I had not read the *first* statute of them, of the King being head of the church. Whereunto I answered, Yes. Then his Mastership declared unto me, that sith it was now by act of parliament ordained, that his highness and his heirs be, and ever of right have been, and perpetually should be, supreme head in earth of the Church of England under Christ, the King's pleasure was, that those of his council there assembled, should demand mine opinion, and what my mind was therein. Whereunto I answered, that in good faith I had well trusted, that the king's highness would never have commanded any such question to be demanded of me, considering that I ever from the beginning, well and truly from time to time declared my mind unto his highness ; and since that time (I said) unto your Mastership, Master Secretary, also, both by mouth and by writing. And now I have in good faith discharged my mind of all such matters, and neither will dispute kings' titles nor popes' : but the King's true faithful subject I am, and will be, and daily I pray for him, and all his, and for you all that are of his honourable council, and for all the realm. And otherwise than this, I never intend to meddle. Whereunto Master Secretary answered, that he thought this manner of answer should not satisfy nor content the king's highness, but that his grace would exact a more full answer. And his Mastership added thereunto that the king's highness was a prince, not of rigour, but of mercy and pity. And though that he had found obstinacy at some time in any of his subjects, yet

when he should find them at another time comformable and submit themselves, his grace would
show mercy : and that concerning myself, his
highness would be glad to see me take such comfortable ways, as I might be abroad in the world
again among other men, as I have been before.
Whereunto I shortly (after the inward affection of my
mind) answered for a very truth, that I would never
meddle in the world again, to have the world given
me.   And to the remnant of the matter, I answered
in effect as before, showing that I had fully determined with myself, neither to study nor meddle with
any matter of this world, but that my whole study
should be upon the passion of Christ, and mine own
passage out of this world.   Upon this I was commanded to go forth for a while, and after called in
again.   At which time Master Secretary said unto
me, that though I were a prisoner condemned to perpetual prison, yet I was not thereby discharged of
mine obedience and allegiance unto the king's highness.   And thereupon demanded me whether that I
thought that the king's grace might not exact of
me such things as are contained in the statutes, and
upon like pains, as he might upon other men.
Whereto I answered that I would not say the contrary.   Whereunto he said that, likewise as the

king's highness would be gracious to them that he found comformable, so his grace would follow the course of his laws toward such as he shall find obstinate. And his Mastership said further, that my demeanour in this matter was a thing that of likelihood made others so stiff therein as they be. Whereto I answered, that I give no man occasion to hold any point one or other, nor never gave any man advice or counsel therein one way or other. And for conclusion I could no farther go, whatsoever pain should come thereof. I am (quoth I) the king's true faithful subject and daily bedesman, and pray for his highness and all the realm. I do nobody no harm, I say none harm, I think none harm, but wish everybody good. And if this be not enough to keep a man alive, in good faith I long not to live. And I am dying already, and have since I came here, been divers times in the case that I thought to die within one hour. And I thank our Lord that I was never sorry for it, but rather sorry when I saw the pang past. And therefore my poor body is at the king's pleasure. Would God my death might do him good. After this Master Secretary said : Well, ye find no fault in that statute : find you any in any of the other statutes after ? Whereto I answered, Sir, whatsoever thing should seem to me other than good, in any of the other statutes or in that statute either, I would not declare what fault I found, nor speak thereof. Whereunto finally his Mastership said, full gently, that of anything that I had spoken here should none advantage be taken. And whether he said farther that there was none to be taken, I am not well remembered. But he said that report should be made unto the king's highness, and his gracious pleasure known. Whereupon I was delivered again to Master Lieutenant, which was then called in. And so was I by Master Lieutenant brought again into my chamber. And here am I yet in such case as I was, neither better nor worse. That that shall follow lieth in the hand of God, Whom I beseech to put in the king's grace's mind, that thing that may be to His high pleasure, and in mine, to mind only the weal of my soul, with little regard of my body, and you with all yours, and my wife, and all my children, and all our other friends, both bodily and ghostly, heartily well to fare. And I pray you and them all pray for me, and take no thought whatsoever shall happen me. For I verily trust in the goodness of God, seem it never so evil to this world, it shall indeed in another world be for the best.

Your loving Father,

THOMAS MORE, Knight.

LETTER VIII

Another Letter written and sent by Sir THOMAS MORE *to his Daughter, Mistress* ROPER, *written in the Year of our Lord,* 1535, *and in the* 27th *Year of the Reign of King* HENRY VIII.

Our Lord bless you and all yours.

FORASMUCH (dearly beloved daughter) as it is likely that you either have heard, or shortly shall hear, that the council were here this day, and that I was before them, I have thought it necessary to send you word how the matter standeth, and verily, to be short, I perceive little difference between this time and the last. For as far as I can see the whole purpose is, either to drive me to say precisely the t'one way, or else precisely the tother. Here sat my Lord of Canterbury, my Lord Chancellor, my Lord of Suffolk, my Lord of Wiltshire, and Master Secretary. And after my coming, Master Secretary made rehearsal in what wise he had reported unto the king's highness, what had been said by his grace's council to me, and what had been answered by me to them at mine other being before them here last. Which thing his Mastership rehearsed, in good faith, very well, as I acknowledged and confessed and heartily thanked him therefore. Whereupon he added thereunto, that the king's highness was nothing content nor satisfied with mine answer, but thought that, by my demeanour, I had been occasion of much grudge and harm in the realm, and that I had an obstinate mind and an evil toward him, and that my duty was, being his subject (and so he had sent them now in his name upon mine allegiance to command me) to make a plain and a terminate answer whether I thought the statute lawful or not. And that I should either acknowledge and confess it lawful, that his highness should be supreme head of the church of England, or else utter plainly my malignity. Whereto I answered that I had no malignity, and therefore I could none utter. And as to the matter I could none other answer make than I had before made, which answer his Mastership had there rehearsed. Very heavy I was that the king's highness should have any such opinion of me. Howbeit if there were one that had informed his highness many evil things of me that were untrue, to which his highness for the time gave credence, I would be very sorry that he should have that opinion of me the space of one day. Howbeit if I were sure that other should come on the morrow, by whom his grace should know the truth of mine innocency, I should in the meanwhile comfort myself with consideration of that. And in likewise now, though it be great heaviness to me, that his highness hath such opinion of me for the while, yet have I no remedy to help it, but only to comfort myself with this consideration that I know very well that the time shall come when God shall declare my truth toward his grace before him and all the world. And whereas it might haply seem to be but small cause of comfort, because I might take harm here first in the meanwhile, I thanked God that my case was such here in this matter, through the clearness of mine own conscience, that though I might have pain, I could not have harm. For a man may in such a case lese his head and have no harm. For I was very sure that I had no corrupt affection, but that I had always from the beginning truly used myself, looking first upon God, and next upon the king, according to the lesson that 'his highness taught me at my first coming to his noble service, the most virtuous lesson that ever prince taught his servant,' whose highness to have of me now such opinion is my great heaviness. But I have no means, as I said, to help it, but only comfort myself in the meantime with the hope of that joyful day in which my truth toward him shall well be known. And in this matter further I could not go, nor other answer thereto I could not make. To this it was said by my Lord Chancellor and Master Secretary both, that the king might by his laws compel me to make a plain answer thereto, either the t'one way or the tother. Whereto I answered that I would not dispute the king's authority, what his highness might do in such a case. But I said that verily, under correction, it seemed to me somewhat hard. For if it so were that my conscience gave me against the statute (wherein how my conscience giveth me I make no declaration) then I, nothing doing nor nothing saying against the statute, it were a very hard thing, to compel me to say, either precisely with it against my conscience to the loss of my soul, or precisely against it to the destruction of my body. To this Master Secretary said, that I had ere this when I was Chancellor, examined heretics and thieves, and other malefactors, and gave me a great praise above my deserving in that behalf. And he said that I then, as he thought, and at the leastwise bishops, did use to examine heretics, whether they believed the

Pope to be head of the church, and used to compel them to make a precise answer thereto. And why should not then the king, since it is a law made here that his grace is head of the church here, compel men to answer precisely to the law here, as they did then concerning the Pope? I answered and said, that I protested that I intended not to defend my part, or stand in contention. But I said there was a difference between those two cases, because that at that time, as well here as elsewhere through the corps of Christendom, the Pope's power was recognised for an undoubted thing; which seemeth not like a thing agreed in this realm, and the contrary taken for truth in other realms. Whereto Master Secretary answered, that they were as well burned for the denying of that, as they be beheaded for the denying of this; and therefore as good reason to compel them to make precise answer to the t'one as to the tother. Whereto I answered, that sith in this case a man is not by a law of one realm so bound in his conscience, where there is a law of the whole corps of Christendom to the contrary in matter touching belief, as he is by a law of the whole corps, though there hap to be made in some place a law local to the contrary, the reasonableness or the unreasonableness in binding a man to precise answer, standeth not in the respect or difference between heading and burning, but because of the difference in charge of conscience, the difference standeth between heading and hell. Much was there answered unto this, both by Master Secretary and my Lord Chancellor, over long to rehearse. And in conclusion they offered me an oath, by which I should be sworn, to make true answer to such things as should be asked me on the king's behalf, concerning the king's own person. Whereto I answered, 'that verily I never purposed to swear any book oath more while I lived.' Then they said that I was very obstinate if I would refuse that, for every man doth it in the star chamber and everywhere. I said that was true, but I had not so little foresight, but that I might well conjecture what should be part of mine interrogatories ; and as good it was to refuse them at the first as afterward. Whereto my Lord Chancellor answered, that he thought I guessed truth, for I should see them. And so they were showed me, 'and they were but twain ; the first, whether I had seen the statute '; the tother, ' whether I believed that it were a lawful made statute or not.' Whereupon I refused the oath, said further by mouth that the first I had before confessed, and to the second I would make none answer ; which was the end of our communication, and I was thereupon sent away. In the communication before, it was said that it was marvelled that I stake so much in my conscience, while at the uttermost I was not sure therein. Whereto I said that I was very sure that mine own conscience, so informed as it is, by such diligence as I have so long taken therein, may stand with mine own salvation. 'I meddle not with the conscience of them that think otherwise.' Every man *suo damno stat aut cadit*. I am no man's judge. It was also said unto me, that if I had as lief be out of the world as in it, as I had there said, why did I not then speak even plain out against the statute? It appeared well I was not content to die, though I said so. Whereto I answered, as the truth is, that I have not been a man of such holy living, as I might be bold to offer myself to death, lest God for my presumption might suffer me to fall, and therefore I put not myself forward but draw back. Howbeit, if God draw me to it Himself, then trust I in His great mercy that He shall not fail to give me grace and strength. In conclusion Master Secretary said, that he liked me this day much worse than he did the last time. For then he said he pitied me much, and now he thought I meant not well. But God and I know both that I mean well, and so I pray God do by me. I pray you, be you and mine other good friends of good cheer whatso-

ver fall of me, and take no thought for me, but pray
or me, as I do and shall for you and all them.

Your tender loving Father,
THOMAS MORE, Knight.

LETTER IX

Sir THOMAS MORE *was beheaded at the Tower-hill, in* LONDON, *on* TUESDAY, *the sixth day of* JULY, *in the year of our Lord* 1535, *and in the xxvii. year of the Reign of King* HENRY VIII. *And on the day next before, being* MONDAY, *and the fifth day of* JULY, *he wrote with a coal a letter to his daughter Mistress* ROPER, *and sent it to her (which was the last thing that ever he wrote), the copy whereof here followeth.*

OUR Lord bless you, good daughter, and your good husband, and your little boy, and all yours, and all my children, and all my god-children and all our friends. Recommend me, when ye may to my good daughter *Cicily*, whom I beseech our Lord to comfort. And I send her my blessing, and to all her children, and pray her to pray for me. I send her an handkerchief: and God comfort my good son her husband. My good daughter *Dance* hath the picture in parchment, that you delivered me from my Lady

Coniers, her name is on the backside. Show her that I heartily pray her, that you may send it in my name to her again, for a token from me to pray for me. I like special well *Dorothy Coly*, I pray you be good unto her. I would wit whether this be she that you wrote me of. If not, yet I pray you be good to the tother, as you may in her affliction, and to my good daughter *Joan Aleyn* too. Give her, I pray you, some kind answer, for she sued hither to me this day to pray you be good to her. I cumber you, good *Margaret*, much, but I would be sorry if it should be any longer than to morrow. For it is Saint Thomas' Eve, and the Utas of Saint Peter : and therefore to-morrow long I to go to God : it were a day very meet and convenient for me. I never liked your manner toward me better than when you kissed me last : for I love when daughterly love and dear charity hath no leisure to look to worldly courtesy. Fare-well, my dear child, and pray for me, and I shall for you and all your friends, that we may merrily meet in heaven. I thank you for your great cost. I send now to my good daughter *Clement* her algorism stone, and I send her, and my godson, and all hers God's blessing and mine. I pray you at time con-venient recommend me to my good son *John More*. I liked well his natural fashion. Our Lord bless him and his good wife my loving daughter, to whom I pray him to be good, as he hath great cause : and that if the land of mine come to his hand, he break not my will concerning his sister *Dance*. And our Lord bless *Thomas* and *Austen* and all that they shall have.

EPITAPHS

Sir THOMAS MORE *being Lord Chancellor of* ENGLAND *gave over that Office, by his great suit and labour, the* 16 *day of May,* A.D. 1532, *and in the* 24*th year of the reign of King* HENRY VIII. *And after in that summer he wrote an epitaph in Latin and caused it to be written upon his tomb of stone which himself, while he was Lord Chancellor, had caused to be made in his Parish Church of* CHELSEA, *where he dwelt, three small miles from* LONDON, *the copy of which epitaph here followeth.*

THOMAS MORUS urbe *Londinensi* familia non celebri sed honesta natus, in literis utcunque versatus quum et causas aliquot annos juvenis egisset in foro, et in urbe sua pro Shyrevo jus dixisset, ab invictissimo rege *Henrico* octavo (cui uni regum omnium gloria prius inaudita contigit, ut *Fidei defensor,* qualem et gladio se et calamo vere prestitit, merito vocaretur) adscitus in Aulam est, delectusque in consilium, et creatus eques proquæstor primum, post Cancellarius *Lancastriæ,* tandem *Angliæ* miro Principis favore factus est. Sed

179

interim in publico Regni Senatu lectus est orator Populi ; præterea legatus Regis nonnunquam fuit alias alibi : postremo vero *Cameraci* comes et collega junctus principi legationis *Cuthberto Tunstallo* tum *Londinensi* mox *Dunelmensi* Episcopo, quo viro vix habet orbis hodie quicquam eruditius, prudentius, melius. Ibi inter summos orbis christiani monarchos rursus refecta fœdera redditamque mundo diu desideratam pacem, et lætissimus vidit, et legatus interfuit.

Quam superi pacem firment faxintque perennem. In hoc officiorum vel honorum cursu quum ita versaretur ut neque princeps optimus operam ejus improbaret, neque nobilibus esset invisus, nec injucundus populo, furibus autem, homicidis, hæreticisque molestus, pater ejus [1]tandem *Joannes Morus* eques et in eum Judicum Ordinem a principe cooptatus, qui *regius consessus* vocatur, homo civilis, suavis, innocens, mitis, misericors, æquus et integer, annis quidem gravis, sed corpore plusquam pro ætate vivido, postquam eo productam sibi vitam vidit ut filium videret *Angliæ* Cancellarium, satis in terra jam se moratum ratus, libens emigravit in Cœlum. At filius, defuncto patre, cui quamdiu supererat comparatus et juvenis vocari consueverat, et ipse quoque sibi videbatur, amissum jam patrem requirens, et æditos ex se liberos

[1] A.D. 1518.

180

quatuor ac nepotes undecim respiciens apud animum suum cœpit persenescere. Auxit hunc affectum animi subsecuta statim, velut adpetentis senij signum pectoris valetudo deterior. Itaque mortalium harum rerum satur, quam rem a puero pene semper optaverat, ut ultimos aliquot vitæ suæ annos obtineret liberos, quibus hujus vitæ negotijs paulatim se subducens futuræ posset immortalitatem meditari, eam rem tandem (si cœptis annuat DEUS) indulgentissimi Principis incomparabili beneficio resignatis honoribus impetravit: atque hoc sepulchrum sibi, quod mortis eum nunquam cessantis abrepere quotidie common faceret, translatis huc prioris uxoris ossibus, extruendum curavit. Quod ne superstes frustra sibi fecerit, neve ingruentem trepidus mortem horreat, sed desiderio Christi libens oppetat, mortemque ut sibi non omnino mortem, sed januam vitæ fælicioris inveniat precibus eum piis, lector optime, spirantem precor defunctumque prosequere.

Under this epitaph in prose he caused to be written on his tomb this Latin epitaph in verses following, which himself had made 20[1] *Years before.*

Chara *Thomæ* jacet hic *Joanna* uxorcula *Mori*,
   Qui tumulum *Aliciæ* hunc destino, quique mihi.

[1] 1513.

Una mihi dedit hoc conjuncta virentibus annis,
  Me vocet ut puer et trina puella patrem.
Altera privignis (quæ gloria rara novercæ est)
  Tam pia quam gratis vix fuit ulla suis.
Altera sic mecum vixit, sic altera vivit,
  Charior incertum est, hæc sit an hæc fuerit.
O simul O juncti poteramus vivere nos tres,
  Quam bene si factum religioque sinant.
At societ tumulus, societ nos obsecro cœlum,
  Sic Mors, non potuit quod dare Vita, dabit.

But of this place of rest Sir Thomas had like to
have been disappointed, by his falling under the
King's displeasure and having an untimely death, had
it not been for the piety and interest of his daughter
Mrs. Roper. For after his execution his headless
body being buried by order in St. Peter's chapel
within the Tower, Mrs. Roper got leave, not long
after, to remove her father's corpse to Chelsea, to be
laid where he himself had designed it should rest.

NOTES.

3. *William Roper*, 1496–1578, was sheriff of Kent in 1521, and long time clerk of the pleas of the king's bench. He married in 1525 More's eldest daughter and lived much in his confidence. His wife died in 1544, but he survived till 3 Jan., 1578. The work was apparently written in Queen Mary's time.

5. *St. Anthony's in London.* A free school belonging to the Hospital of St. Anthony in Threadneedle Street, at that time taught by Nicolas Holt, author later of a Latin grammar called *Lac Puerorum*, which contains some of More's epigrams. It was, according to Stow, the best school in London. See Stow, Newcourt.

Oxford. More was there in 1492–3, at Canterbury Hall, afterwards absorbed by Christ Church. He was taught Greek by Linacre.

5. *Cardinal Morton.* See More's description of Morton's household in the *Utopia*.

6. *New Inn.* Now destroyed. It lay on the site of the Aldwych constructed in 1903. More was a member in 1492–3.

6. *Charterhouse.* A Carthusian monastery founded by Sir Walter Manny in 1371.

6. *Master Colte.* More's first wife was Jane (or Joan), daughter of John Colt, of Newhall, Essex. After her death

183

(1511) he married a widow, Alice Middleton, daughter of John More, of Losely, Surrey.

7. *three fifteenths.* The Venetian Ambassador in 1500 says that one-fifteenth of the three estates amounted to £37,930. *Italian relation,* p. 52.

eldest daughter, Margaret, m. James IV. of Scotland, 1502.

7. *three daughters and one son.* Margaret (1505) m. William Roper, Elizabeth (1506) m. William Dancy, and Cecilia (1507) m. Giles Heron, John (1509) m. Anne Cresacre.

7. *called to the Bench ;* i.e. became a bencher. *Reader in Court.* An office reserved for benchers. His first reading was in the autumn of 1511, at Lincoln's Inn, his second in Lent, 1516. He had before been reader in Furnival's Inn.

8. *his father.* John More (sergeant-at-law Nov., 1503, Justice Common Pleas, Nov., 1517, King's Bench April 1520) was a Commissioner for Hertfordshire for the collection of the subsidy.

8. *over sea.* More did, in fact, visit Louvain and Paris in 1508.

8. *Sion.* The monastery of St. Saviour and St. Bridget of Sion at Isleworth, founded by Henry V.

9. *merchants of the Stilliard* were the Flemish merchants of the Hanse. Their house was on the site of Cannon Street Station. They were privileged in 1259, and were governed by their own laws. The "English Merchants" were the Merchant Adventurers' Company, a branch of the Mercers, who received a charter in 1505 to trade with the Low Countries. Their first charter was in 1407. This choice of More took place in 1514. See Gross and Cunningham for details of the Hanse, etc.

10. *the Pope's ambassador.* Cardinal Campeggio.

11. *traverse.* First a screen, then a cross bench, and then any private seat or room screened by a traverse.

into the leads. On the roof.

12. *treasurer of the Exchequer.* It was while More held this office that Tunstall dedicated to him his treatise " *de arte supputandi,*" the first Arithmetic printed in England.

19. *sith.* Since.

27. *no mastery.* Mastery is *magisterium*—a masterpiece—a thing requiring great skill.

29. *sweating sickness.* This disease appeared first in 1485, then in 1508, 1517, 1528, and 1551, when it appeared for the last time. See *Social England,* II. 755 seq. for an account of its symptoms and spread.

30. *glister.* Clyster.

30. *God's marks* are those symptoms in any disease which betoken certain death. *Cf.* "The marks of the plague commonly called Goddes markes," quoted in 1558, in the N.E.D.

31. *wood.* Wroth, angry, mad.

32. *Longland, Bishop of Lincoln* (1521-1547). This charge seems to have been unfounded.

36. *in a fume.* A fit of anger, an irritable mood. *See* Skelton's *Why come ye not to Court.*

37. *ambassadors to Cambray.* In July, 1529. The peace was concluded Aug. 5.

42. *all-were-it.* Cf. *al*beit, *al*though.

44. *injunctions.* The Equity jurisdiction corrected the rigour of an application of the letter of the law to cases outside its original scope by injunctions to stop proceedings, etc., until the Chancery court was satisfied that justice was done.

48. *my sister More.* Anne Cresacre, who married Sir Thomas More's son.

47. *I had liever.* I would rather.

53. *twenty marks.* £13 6s. 8d. annual value=£160 per annum now, say a capital value of about £2,000. He was earning between £4,000 and £5,000 present value when he entered the royal service.

54. *sadly.* Soberly.

55. *Quia spicula prævisa minus lædunt.* Foreseen griefs wound the less.

59. *certain nun.* Elizabeth Barton, the "holy maid of Kent." Executed at Tyburn, April, 1534.

61. *Wiltshire.* Sir Thomas Boleyn (1477-1539), Earl of Wiltshire, father of Anne Boleyn.

185

62. *angels.* A gold coin, at this time coined to be worth about 7s. 6d. (present value £4 10s. 0d. in purchasing power).

62. *instant.* Imperative.

63. *for tediousness omitting.* " For fear of tediousness omitting." A latinism.

64. *misprision of treason* is the bare knowledge and concealment of treason without any degree of assent thereto, for any assent makes the party a traitor.

66. *a book of the assertion.* This was the " Assertio septem sacramentorum adversus Martinum Lutherum," etc. London, 1521, 4to, etc.

67. *Statute of Præmunire,* imposed 1353 and again in 1392. By preventing the recognition of any foreign jurisdiction in England it became a powerful weapon in the hands of Henry VIII.

70. *Indignatio principis mors est.* The wrath of the prince is death.

70. *Quod differtur non aufertur.* What is put off is not done away with.

71. *to appear at Lambeth.* April 13, 1534. The Act had been passed on March 30.

71. *be houseled.* Received the Communion.
rounded me in the ear. Whispered me.

72. *not to be acknown.* Not to be recognizable from the other.

72. *Sir Richard Cromwell.* This name is variously given as Sir Richard Southwell and Sir Richard Winkefield.

75. *a wanton.* A pet. Cf. " Like little wanton boys that swim on bladders."

76. *first statute.* 26 H. VIII. March 30, 1534.
another statute. " When Parliament met on 3 November, 1534, it was voted that the oath as administered to More and Fisher was to be reputed the very oath intended by the act of succession."—*D.N.B.*

77. *contrary to the order of law.* More's goods were forfeit owing to his refusal to take the oath, but the effect of the conveyances was that they were no longer his.

78. *Master Reynolds.* Richard Reynolds, executed May 4, 1535, beatified at the same time as More.

79. *silly.* Weak, frail.

79. These verses are printed in the "Works" of More, p. 1432, and are there called "Lewys the lost lover." See a fuller discussion in the preface.

81. *What the good-yere.* A favourite phrase. See *Merry Wives of Windsor*, I. 4. *Much Ado about Nothing*, I. 3.

81. *muse.* Wonder.

82. *fondly.* Foolishly. *Tylle valle, Tylle valle.* First line of a popular song, occurs in *Twelfth Night*, II. 3., 2 *Henry IV.*, II. 4., Skelton, Gower, etc.

84. *Statute.* 26 H. VIII. c. 13. Nov. 18, 1534.

88. *Quia si dixerimus.* "If we say that we have no sin, we deceive ourselves, and the truth is not in us." 1 John i. 8.

to temporal man before. More was the first layman to be Lord High Chancellor.

92. *St. Paul said to the Corinthians.* 1 Corinthians iv. 15.

95. *merrily.* With good cheer.

Old Swan. The landing place west of London Bridge, still in existence as a pier.

96. More's trial and condemnation took place July 1st, 1535.

98. *Utas of St. Peter.* The Octave of St. Peter and the Eve of the Translation of St. Thomas a Becket.

100. *javill.* Javel, a worthless fellow.

105. *secretly.* In private, silently.

108. *played their pageant.* In the old town plays each company came in turn to every platform, played their pageant, or share of the plays, and went on to the next stand. The word was also used for a series of emblematic charades or even pictures. More himself had designed some of these last, and written verses for them.

110. *soyleth.* Assoileth.

114. *Æsop's fables.* On p. 124 this is referred to Wolsey.

123. *sely.* Simpleton.

130. *let* in line 3=delay. At the foot of the page=allow.

Pie. The court of Piepowder. A court of summary jurisdiction in fairs, presided over by the bailiff of the Lord of the Manor, or other holder of the tolls.

131. *escheator.* An officer appointed to take note of the escheats and forfeitures in his district, and to report them to the Exchequer.

tolling. Dragging.

quests'. The jurors and bailiff formed the " inquest."

cast. Condemn in costs.

132. *wonnest.* Gettest to.

146. *lewdness.* Ignorance, folly.

154. *Nam in manu, etc.* For the heart of the king is in the hand of God, etc.

158. *namely.* Especially.

171. *corps.* Body.

176. *algorism stone.* Probably a slate ruled in columns to work simple sums in arithmetic on.

182. These are extracted from Weaver's *Funeral Monuments*, pp. 505-6.

BIBLIOGRAPHICAL NOTE.

WILLIAM ROPER'S LIFE.

(1). The Mirrour of Vertue in worldly greatness, or the life of Syr Thomas More, Knight, sometime Lord Chancellour. Edited by T.P. (? Thomas Plowden). Paris, 1626. 12mo (B.M.).

(2) Edited by Thomas Hearne, Oxford, 1716, 8vo (B.M.).
(3) Edited by John Lewis, London, 1729, 8vo (B.M.).
(4)   The same   London, 1731, 8vo (B.M.).
(5)   The same   Dublin, 1765, 8vo (Singer).
(6) Edited by Singer, London, 1817, 8vo (B.M.), only 150 copies.
(7)   The same   London, 1822, 8vo (B.M.).
(8) Lewis, Dublin, 1835, 8vo (B.M.) (7th Edition).
(9) Hearne-Lumby, Cambridge, 1879, 8vo (B.M.), with the *Utopia*.
(10) Hearne-Adams, London, 1886, 8vo (B.M.), with the *Utopia*.
(11) Singer-Gollancz, London, fol.

MSS. in the British Museum.   Harleian 6166, 6254, 6362, 7030.

THOMAS STAPLETON'S LIFE IN "TRES THOMAE."
(1) Douai, 1588, 8vo (B.M.).
(2) Cologne, 1612, 8vo (B.M.).
(3) Paris, 1620, fol. (B.M.).
(4) Cologne, 1689, fol., in collected Works of More.
(5) Gratz, 1689, 8vo (B.M.).
(6) Liege, 1849, 8vo (B.M.) (a French translation).

CRESACRE MORE'S LIFE.
(1) Paris? 1626, 4to (B.M.).   (? London).
(2) London, 1642, 4to.
(3) London, 1726, 8vo (B.M.).
(4) Leipzig, 1741, 8vo (Oellinger).   A German translation.
(5) Edited by Joseph Hunter, London, 1828, 8vo (B.M.).

J. Hoddesdon's *History of the Life and Death of More*, London, 1652, 8vo (B.M.).   Another Edition, 1662 12mo (Oellinger).

INDEX.

ing the future

Made in the USA
Lexington, KY
30 September 2012